The Power of Woman

The Power of Woman

The Life and Writings of

Sarah Moore Grimké

℘

Pamela R. Durso

Mercer University Press
Macon, Georgia

ISBN 0-86554-876-5
MUP/P281

First Edition.

Library of Congress Cataloging-in-Publication Data

Durso, Pamela R.
 The power of woman : the life and writings of Sarah Moore Grimké /
Pamela R. Durso.-- 1st ed.
    p. cm.
Includes bibliographical references and index.
 ISBN 0-86554-876-5 (hardcover : alk. paper)
1. Grimkâe, Sarah Moore, 1792-1873. 2. Women in
Christianity—Biography. 3. Feminist theology. 4. Women
abolitionists—South Carolina—Biography.
5. Feminists—South Carolina—Biography. I. Title.
 BV639.W7D87 2003
 326'.092—dc22

                                                        2003020863

To Dr. William Pitts, my teacher, my mentor, and my friend.
Thank you for your encouragement and help
as I was completing my dissertation on Sarah Grimké,
and thank you for your continued support through the years.

To Dr. Keith Durso, my husband, my proofreader,
and my faithful encourager.
Thank you for all you have done in the past twelve years to
make this book a reality. I could not have done it without you.

Contents

Preface

Born in Charleston, South Carolina, to a slave-owning family, Sarah Moore Grimké developed a strong disdain for slavery at an early age. She eventually left her home and her family and moved to Philadelphia. In the late 1830s, she began attacking slavery publicly and went on to become one of the first female agents of the American Anti-Slavery Society. She also became one of the earliest women in the antislavery movement who addressed audiences composed of men and women and was among the first women abolitionists to defend the right of women to move outside their traditional role. Sarah was a vocal and powerful advocate of full equality for women in all areas of life. Her work and her contributions are astounding, given that she was not allowed the education she desired and never had the opportunity to pursue a full-time, lifelong career. Sarah lived in a world that placed limits on her abilities and her desires, yet she did not surrender to those limits. Instead, she became an agent for change and helped to re-create the nature of female activism in the United States.

My first awareness of Sarah Grimké came in 1989 during a graduate history seminar with Dr. Stanley Campbell at Baylor University, and I am grateful Dr. Campbell for introducing me to the women of the abolition movement. In 1990, when I decided to make Sarah the topic of my dissertation, Dr. William L. Pitts, professor of church history at Baylor University and director of my dissertation committee, encouraged my interest in Sarah. I am thankful for his support, kindness, and attention to detail. His guidance and suggestions remain evident in this "new and improved" version of my dissertation. I am also indebted to my husband, Keith Durso. During the dissertation stage and again during the revision stage of this book, his work as a careful proofreader and an insightful critic enhanced the writing and analysis found in this book, and I am grateful for his continual encouragement and assistance.

During the dissertation stage of writing, the librarians at the William L. Clements Library of the University of Michigan provided great help in directing me to and providing me with the diaries of Sarah Grimké, which are housed in their library's microfilm collection. I am also grateful to Derek Hogan, theologian librarian at Campbell University, who solved footnote problems for me during the final stage of writing.

I am most grateful to my parents, Mac and Lorita Robinson, who have continually encouraged my dreams and supported my pursuits. And finally, I am thankful for my children, Michael and Alexandra. They are completely unimpressed that Mom has written a book, but they both view the world as a place of unlimited opportunities and possibilities, and thus they are in many ways beneficiaries of the work of Sarah Grimké.

Chapter 1

"The Power of Woman"

The Importance of Sarah Grimké

The nineteenth century was a time of expansion, turmoil, advancement, and reform in the United States. The Industrial Revolution changed the daily lives of all Americans as the country moved from an agrarian to an urban society complete with cities, factories, and monopolies. As these changes were occurring, a series of revivals that would develop into the Second Great Awakening began. Before the revivals were underway, women constituted a large majority of church members, and they became a vital force in carrying out the work of the revivals. They initiated many of the meetings, held prayer groups, and organized maternal associations, missionary societies, and fundraising boards. The women also brought their husbands and children to the revivals and thus provided new candidates for conversion at the meetings.[1]

Many of the middle-class women who involved themselves in the revival movement had much free time, and they used this time to

---

[1]George M. Thomas, *Revivalism and Cultural Change: Christianity, Nation Building, and the Market in the Nineteenth Century United States* (Chicago/London: University of Chicago Press, 1989) 71.

support and further a wide variety of faith-based reform efforts. They devoted themselves to ending evils such as alcohol abuse, slavery, prostitution, war, poverty, and violence against women, children, and prisoners. This great interest and involvement in reform work was the foundation of the rise of the Benevolence Empire, a network of reform societies and movements.[2] This empire was based upon the voluntary work of individuals, mostly women, who desired the betterment of their society.[3]

The abolitionist movement of the 1830s began during this time of great reform. Those involved in abolition work believed themselves to have a "sacred vocation," a divine cause. They worked for the abolition of slavery with the fervor of true reformers, and a large percentage of these workers were women. The work the women did as abolitionists was consistent with the work they did in other benevolent efforts. They organized separate female antislavery societies in order to support men's organizations, and they focused attention on the female victims and domestic casualties of slavery. Unlike other reform movements of the day, however, abolitionism had an unavoidably political thrust and a tendency to outgrow its

---

[2]The development of a market economy, the advances in political democracy, the rapid increase in social and geographic mobility, and the impact of the Second Great Awakening all contributed to the organization of a large number of charitable and reform associations in the 1830s. See Beverly Wildung Harrison, "The Early Feminists and the Clergy: A Case Study in the Dynamics of Secularization," *Review and Expositor* 72 (1975): 41–52; Nancy A. Hewitt, "Feminist Friends: Agrarian Quakers and the Emergence of Woman's Rights in America," *Feminist Studies* 12/1 (Spring 1986): 27–49; Carroll Smith Rosenberg, "Beauty, the Beast and the Militant Woman: A Case Study in Sex Roles and Social Stress in Jacksonian America," *American Quarterly* 23/4 (October 1971): 562–84; and Mary P. Ryan, "The Power of Women's Networks: A Case Study of Female Moral Reform in Antebellum America," *Feminist Studies* 5/1 (Spring 1979): 66–86.

[3]Nancy Hardesty, *Women Called to Witness: Evangelical Feminism in the Nineteenth Century*, 2d. ed. (Knoxville: University of Tennessee Press, 1999) 21.

religious origins. As the movement secularized, so did the activities of its female members.[4] Thus, the abolition crusade was for women the most controversial, most political, and most effective of all the reform movements of the time.[5]

One woman instrumental in revolutionizing the role of women in the abolition movement was Sarah Moore Grimké. Sarah's lifelong goal was to become "a useful member of society."[6] From childhood on, she possessed a passionate desire to learn, to participate fully in life, and to contribute to the well-being of others. Yet she continually struggled to meet her goal. Familial, religious, and societal restrictions hampered her attempts at being useful. Despite these restrictions, Sarah contributed greatly: first to the cause of abolition and later to the cause of women's rights.

Sarah was not the first woman to write or speak against slavery, nor was she the first to insist that women had the right to lecture publicly. Sarah and her sister, Angelina Emily Grimké,[7] however, were the first women from a Southern slave-owning family to attack slavery publicly, the first women to act as agents of the American Anti-Slavery Society, the first women in the antislavery movement to address audiences composed of men and women, and the first women abolitionists to defend the right of women to move outside their traditional sphere. Together, the

---

[4]Ellen Carol DuBois, *Feminism and Suffrage: The Emergence of an Independent Women's Movement in America, 1848–1869* (Ithaca: Cornell University Press, 1978) 32–33.

[5]Keith E. Melder, *Beginning of Sisterhood: The American Woman's Rights Movement, 1800–1850,* Studies in the Life of Women, ed. Gerda Lerner (New York: Shocken Books, 1977) 49, 56.

[6] Sarah Grimké, "The Education of Women," in *Letters on the Equality of the Sexes and Other Essays*, ed., Elizabeth Ann Bartlett (New Haven: Yale University Press, 1988) 114.

[7]The lives and work of Sarah and Angelina Grimké were closely intertwined, and to provide a comprehensive study of Sarah, Angelina's activities and writings must also be examined. To avoid confusion, therefore, the first names of the sisters will be used throughout the book.

Grimké sisters helped to change the nature of female activism in the United States.

In the late 1830s when the Grimké sisters were at the height of their popularity, the younger sister, Angelina, received the majority of attention, which may be attributed to two factors. First, she was the better speaker, and second, she married Theodore Dwight Weld, one of the most prominent abolitionists of the day. She continues to be the more celebrated of the two sisters with the bulk of scholarly attention being focused on her life and writings.[8]

Sarah, along with Angelina, has been the subject of two major biographies.[9] In 1885, Catherine H. Birney, an ardent and loving friend of both sisters, wrote the first biography: *The Grimké Sisters, Sarah and Angelina Grimké: The First American Women Advocates of Abolition and Woman's Rights.*[10] Birney had complete access to

---

[8]Scholarly works devoted primarily to the life and work of Angelina include: Charles Wilbanks, ed. *Walking by Faith: The Diary of Angelina Grimké, 1828–1835, Women's Diaries and Letters of the South* (Columbia: University of South Carolina Press, 2003); Stephen Howard Browne, *Angelina Grimké: Rhetoric, Identity, and the Radical Imagination, Rhetoric and Public Affairs Series* (East Lansing: Michigan State University Press, 2000); Katharine Du Pre Lumpkin, *The Emancipation of Angelina Grimké* (Chapel Hill: University of North Carolina Press, 1974); Jean Fagan Yellin, "Angelina Grimké," *Women and Sisters: The Antislavery Feminists in American Culture* (New Haven: Yale University Press, 1989) 29–52; Phyllis M. Japp, "Esther or Isaiah?: The Abolitionist-Feminist Rhetoric of Angelina Grimké," *Quarterly Journal of Speech* 71/3 (August 1985): 335–48; and Mary E. Vielhaber, "An Abandoned Speaking Career: Angelina Grimké," *Michigan Academician* 17/1 (Spring 1984): 59–66.

[9]A biography of the sisters has been written for children: Stephanie Sammartino McPherson, *Sisters Against Slavery: A Story about Sarah and Angelina Grimké, Creative Minds Biographies* (Minneapolis: Carolrhoda Books, 1999). Another children's book has been written about the life of Angelina: Ellen H. Todras, *Angelina Grimké: Voice of Abolition* (North Haven CT: Linnet Books, 1999).

[10]Catherine H. Birney, *Sarah and Angelina Grimké: The First American Women Advocates of Abolition and Woman's Rights* (North

the Grimkés' diaries and letters, making her book extraordinarily helpful. Her account is an affectionate tribute to Sarah and Angelina, lacking in professional documentation and in any objective analysis of the sisters' reform efforts.

Gerda Lerner wrote the second biography in 1967, titled *The Grimké Sisters from South Carolina: Rebels Against Slavery.*[11] It is the most thorough, objective, and critical account of the lives and work of the Grimkés, yet its author only briefly mentions and offers no analysis of Sarah Grimké's greatest achievement—*Letters on the Equality of the Sexes.* Lerner also underestimates the depth of Sarah's religious commitment by assuming that reform was the essence of, rather than an outward manifestation of, that commitment. Finally, in Lerner's biography, as is true of most other writings about the Grimké sisters, Angelina is the dominant figure, and less attention is given to the life, work, and contributions of Sarah. The lack of attention is especially true with regard to Sarah's later life and writings. Lerner rectified some of these weaknesses in the 1998 publication of *The Feminist Thought of Sarah Grimké,* which focuses primarily on Sarah and includes several of her letters and later manuscripts.

Lerner, now Professor of History, *Emerita,* at the University of Wisconsin, is, however, candid about her inability to understand Sarah's theological basis for her reform efforts. Lerner wrote in the introduction to the 1998 book, "Sarah's argument for the emancipation of women was almost entirely theological; her language was biblical; her images were derived from Christian iconography. I was not trained in theology and had only a cursory knowledge of Christian thought; thus I found it difficult to

---

Carolina: Lee and Shepard, 1885; reprint, Westport CT: Greenwood Press, 1969).

[11]Gerda Lerner, *The Grimké Sisters From South Carolina: Pioneers for Woman's Rights and Abolition,* Studies in the Life of Women, ed. Gerda Lerner (New York: Schocken Books, 1971).

comprehend her arguments."[12] Lerner's further research demonstrates that she has attempted to understand Sarah's writings in the context of her Christian faith, yet in writing as a non-believer about the faith basis of Sarah's reform, Lerner has failed to capture Sarah's faith as the driving force behind her reform work.

The lack of a biography centered solely on the life and writings of Sarah Grimké is what led to the writing of this book. My interest in Sarah began as a graduate student. In a Civil War Seminar, I was asked to write a paper about female abolitionists and to offer some insight as to whether their commitment to abolition stemmed from their feminist leanings or whether their feminism was a direct result of their participation in the antislavery reform. In the writing of the paper, I discovered Sarah and Angelina Grimké. As I read their writings and pondered their contributions, I felt more drawn to Sarah. She, in many ways, had lived out some of my own struggle. Her difficulty in finding a place of ministry and her questioning of traditional biblical interpretations seemed all too relevant to me in 1989, and thus, when it was time to write a dissertation, I knew that Sarah would be the perfect subject for me. Reading her writings and delving into her life struggles, I thought, would provide answers to my own doubts about being called into ministry and would prompt me to reexamine some more difficult scriptural passages and my own understanding of those passages.

After I completed the dissertation in 1992, I put it away and moved on with life commitments. Four years ago, I began my teaching career at a Baptist divinity school, and in the past few years, I have completed more research on Sarah and have presented her story to church groups, divinity school classes, and women's meetings. Part of what has motivated me to write this book on Sarah is the interest in and fascination with Sarah that my audience members have demonstrated. Men and women alike have responded to stories about Sarah with great interest. They listened to the story

---

[12]Gerda Lerner, *The Feminist Thought of Sarah Grimké* (New York/Oxford: Oxford University Press, 1998) 5.

of a woman who faced rejection because of her view of ministry and her biblical interpretation. Her story resonates with the women, many of whom are in ministry or are contemplating their call to ministry. These women identified with Sarah's description of the person called to ministry, a person who has a passionate desire and an almost inescapable drive to preach the gospel message, and members of my audience also understood Sarah's poignant words about women who have keep their calling suppressed rather than face sure hostility and rejection. Sarah wrote of this desire and of the restrictions often encountered by women in her best known writing, *Letters on the Equality of the Sexes*:

It is truly marvellous that any woman can rise above the pressure of circumstances which combine to crush her. Nothing can strengthen her to do this in the character of a preacher of righteousness, but a call from Jehovah himself. And when the voice of God penetrates the deep recesses of her heart, and commands her to go and cry in the ears of the people, she is ready to exclaim, "Ah, Lord God, behold I cannot speak, for I am a woman." I have known women in different religious societies, who have felt like the prophet. "His word was in my heart as a burning fire shut up in my bones, and I was weary with forbearing." But they have not dared to open their lips, and have endured all the intensity of suffering, produced by disobedience to God, rather than encounter heartless ridicule and injurious suspicions. I rejoice that we have been the oppressed, rather than the oppressors. God thus prepared his people for deliverance from outward bondage; and I hope our sorrows have prepared us to fulfil our high and holy duties, whether public or private, with humility and meekness; and that suffering has imparted fortitude to endure trials, which assuredly await us in attempt to sunder those chains with which man has bound us, galling to the spirit, though unseen by the eye.[13]

Reading words such as these has convinced me that Sarah's life and writings are as relevant today as they were in the 1830s and that there is a need in our society and in today's churches to hear her words and to know of her contributions to her world and to ours.

For me, the compelling factor in Sarah's story is that all her work and writings grew out of the depth of her own religious commitment. She believed that:

> The motto of woman, when she is engaged in the great work of public reformation should be,—'The Lord is my light and my salvation; whom shall I fear? The Lord is the strength of my life; of whom shall I be afraid?' She must feel, if she feels rightly, that she is fulfilling one of the important duties laid upon her as an accountable being, and that her character, instead of being unnatural,' is in exact accordance with the will of Him to whom, and to no other, she is responsible for the talents and the gifts confided to her.[14]

This faith commitment led Sarah to work tirelessly for societal and individual reform, and much of her work was done in areas in which we as Americans and as Christians continue to struggle. Sarah attacked slavery and racial prejudice. She reevaluated the religious restrictions placed on women by the church. She offered a new interpretation of scripture that challenged gender biases and defended women's involvement in ministry. She countered the view that "the power of woman is in her dependence" on man with the view that the power of woman lay in her willingness to petition God

---

[13]Sarah Grimké, *Letters on the Equality of the Sexes and Other Essays,* ed. Elizabeth Ann Bartlett (New Haven: Yale University Press, 1988) 88.

[14]Ibid., 41.

to lead her in truth and then to teach that truth to others, thereby leading "souls to Christ, and not to Pastors for instruction."[15]

Sarah's work in the abolition movement and her writings about the equality of women resulted in her being a role model for a younger generation of women who would become the leaders of the suffrage movement, and I believe that she continues to serve as a role model for all women who desire vocational, educational, legal, and financial equality. Sarah's contributions were many, her influence was lasting, and her life truly was "useful."

---

[15]Ibid., 39, 40.

Chapter 2

The Formative Years and Experiences

of Sarah Grimké

The unwavering determination and self-reliance Sarah Grimké displayed throughout her life may be attributed at least in part to the strong family into which she was born. She was born on 26 November 1792 in Charleston, South Carolina, the sixth child and second daughter of John and Mary Grimké.

Sarah's father, John Faucheraud Grimké, was a man of high political and social standing in his state. His place among the ruling elite of South Carolina stemmed from his family heritage as well as from his own intellectual distinction and enterprising nature. Grimké's maternal relations, the Faucherauds, were among the Huguenots who fled France en mass in 1685 when Louis XIV revoked the Edict of Nantes, which ended religious freedom for Protestants in that region. The Faucherauds came to America and settled in Charleston in 1686.[1] By the mid-eighteenth century, the Faucherauds were one of the established families of South Carolina.

---

[1]Catherine H. Birney, *Sarah and Angelina Grimké: The First American Women Advocates of Abolition and Woman's Rights* (Lee and Shepard, 1885; reprint, Westport CT: Greenwood Press, 1969) 5.

The first Grimké to arrive in America was Frederick Grimké, a native of Germany who emigrated to South Carolina in 1733. He acquired a plantation soon after his arrival, but his primary concern was running a mercantile business. He dealt in imported rum, molasses, household goods, and African slaves.[2] Frederick Grimké's younger brother John Paul arrived in America in 1740, and with Frederick's assistance, he established a thriving business as a master silversmith. The Grimké brothers were hardworking young men determined to acquire property and to move into the elite social circle of Charleston. They achieved their goal when John Paul Grimké married Marie Faucheraud.

John Faucheraud Grimké was born to this moderately wealthy and influential couple on 16 December 1752. Grimké was sent to England for his collegiate studies, but upon the outbreak of the Revolutionary War, he left his studies and returned home. He enlisted in the army and was commissioned as a captain in the South Carolina Continental artillery. Grimké quickly rose through the military ranks and by the end of the war had been promoted to lieutenant colonel. Following the victory of the Revolutionary Army, Grimké returned home and entered politics.

Grimké served five years (1782–1786) in South Carolina's House of Representatives, during which time he held the office of Speaker of the House for one year. At the same time, he held a judgeship to which he was appointed in 1783. In 1788, Grimké served as a member of the state convention that ratified the Federal Constitution and acted as Charleston's mayor.[3] In 1799, he became senior associate of the state's supreme court, which essentially made him chief justice of the highest court in the state. His greatest achievement, however, was as a compiler and analyst of South

---

[2]Adrienne Koch, "The Significance of the Grimké Family," *Maryland Historian* 3/1 (Spring 1972): 62. From 1735 to 1738, Grimké purchased and sold at least two cargoes of African slaves.

[3]W. C. Mallalieu, "Grimké, John Faucheraud," in *Dictionary of American Biography*, ed. Allen Johnson and Dumas Malone (New York: Scribner's and Sons, 1931) 633–34.

Carolina law. In 1790, he privately published 500 copies of *The Public Laws of the State of South Carolina*, a 547-page document that was for several decades the most important work on South Carolina law.[4]

In 1784, Grimké married Mary Smith, the twenty-year-old daughter of the affluent and influential banker Thomas Smith. Her family heritage was even more impressive than that of her husband. Her paternal ancestors included Thomas Smith, the proprietary Governor and Landgrave of South Carolina, two colonial governors and a speaker of the Common House Assembly.[5]

Like her husband, Mary led an active life. She gave birth to fourteen children in a twenty-year span, two of whom died in infancy and one of whom died in early childhood. The remaining children were John, Thomas, Mary, Frederick, Sarah, Anna, Eliza, Benjamin, Henry, Charles, and Angelina. In addition to her duties as a mother, Mary was responsible for the oversight of two households. The Grimkés owned a home on Church Street in Charleston, and they spent their summers in that home. From November to May, the family lived on their Beaufort plantation. Thus, Mary had to supervise the management of two homes, arrange transportation for several moves during the year, and direct the activities and work schedules of her children and a large household staff of slaves.

Despite the time-consuming duties she fulfilled as a mother and wife, Mary was a devout and active Episcopalian and a leader of Charleston's Ladies Benevolent Society. She also gave freely of her time to the poor and needy of the community as well as to the

---

[4]David Duncan Wallace, *South Carolina: A Short History, 1520–1948* (Columbia: University of South Carolina Press, 1951) 416. John Grimké also authored *South Carolina Justice of the Peace and Duty of Executors and Administrators*.

[5]Annie Miller, *Our Family Circle* (Marietta GA: Continental Book Co., 1957) 72–76.

women confined in a nearby prison.[6] The seemingly overwhelming
duties performed by Mary did not prevent this intelligent and
thoughtful woman from finding time to read. She especially enjoyed
theological works, and she apparently spent some time discussing
the content of her reading material with her son Thomas.[7]

It was into this influential and active family that Sarah was
born in 1792. From infancy, her family met her needs and often
indulged her whims. As was the custom among Southern families of
wealth, her parents left much of the daily care and discipline of the
children to the household slaves. The Grimké family assigned the
care of the children to "Mauma," the black nurse who ruled their
lives with a firm but kind hand. "Mauma" offered them affection
and constant availability, unlike their father, a somewhat stern and
forbidding man who was often absent from the Grimké home, or
their mother, a busy woman whose schedule left little time for the
endless questions and demands of her children.

Mary Grimké's hectic schedule alone was not what kept her
from cultivating meaningful relationships with her children. Her
personal nature also hampered such relationships. Despite her pious
works and developed intellect, she was a woman of narrow views
and judgmental attitudes. Her rigid orthodox beliefs apparently kept
her from ever developing a particularly close, affectionate bond with
any of her sons or daughters.[8]

The lack of attention from her parents most likely was
instrumental in Sarah's becoming an independent and self-sufficient
child. Their inattention also drove Sarah, an intelligent and
determined young girl, to seek out her older brother Thomas as a
confidant and companion. Despite the six-year difference in their
ages, they were very close. Their closeness resulted in part from a
common interest in learning. Thomas, the older and more educated
sibling, willingly shared with Sarah the knowledge he had acquired,

---

[6]Katharine Du Pre Lumpkin, *The Emancipation of Angelina Grimké*
(Chapel Hill: University of North Carolina Press, 1974) 6–8.

[7]Birney, *Sarah and Angelina Grimké*, 14.

[8]Ibid., 16.

instructing her about which books she should read and encouraging her as she studied his lessons with him. With Thomas, she studied mathematics, geography, world history, natural science, botany, and Greek.[9] Thus, Sarah obtained an education that was superior to what most girls received in her day.

In 1805, Thomas left home to attend Yale College. He was fortunate enough to study under the president of that school, Timothy Dwight. Thomas's introduction to higher education also served as Sarah's introduction. On his visits home, he acquainted her with many new ideas including the dangers of the Enlightenment and Deism as well as the truths of the Bible.[10] Sarah copied the notes he took during class and wrote out the articles he intended to publish.

These glimpses into the world of learning convinced Sarah that she not only would continue her general education but also would study law and become a lawyer, an aspiration that was seemingly endorsed by her father. Throughout her childhood, Judge Grimké had allowed Sarah to participate in the legal training he gave to his sons. He engaged them in debates and coached them in the skill of preparing cogent arguments. Sarah thrived on these debates and apparently showed more skill than any of her brothers, and Judge Grimké often remarked that if only Sarah had been a boy, she would have been the best jurist in the land.[11] As a result of her interests in the law and her skills as a debater, Sarah secretly began to study the law, hoping that she might someday become that great jurist.

Sarah's aspirations, however, were not to be fulfilled nor were her studies to continue to be unrestricted. When Thomas began serious academic preparation, both of Sarah's parents objected to

---

[9]Mark Perry, *Lift Up Thy Voice: The Grimké Family's Journey from Slaveholders to Civil Rights Leaders* (New York: Viking, 2001) 23–24.

[10]Elizabeth Ann Bartlett, *Liberty, Equality, Sorority: The Origins and Interpretation of American Feminist Thought: Frances Wright, Sarah Grimké, and Margaret Fuller* (Brooklyn NY: Carlson Publishing Inc., 1994) 57.

[11]Birney, *Sarah and Angelina Grimké*, 8.

her desire to continue studying with him. Even Thomas ridiculed Sarah's desire to move beyond the elementary stages of academia. Her earnest pleas for an education were met with, "'You are a girl—what do you want with Latin and Greek etc.? You can never use them, ' accompanied sometimes by a smile, sometimes by a sneer."[12] Without Thomas's approval or help, Sarah's secret dream of becoming a lawyer was stifled. Years later she wrote, "Had I received the education I coveted and been bred to the profession of the law, a dignity to which I secretly aspired, I might have been a useful member of society, and instead of myself and my property being taken care of I might have been a protector of the helpless and the unfortunate, a pleader for the poor and the dumb."[13]

The one bright spot in Sarah's life during these years of being denied the education she so desperately wanted was the birth of her youngest sister. On 20 February 1805, just a few weeks after Thomas left home for college, Sarah's mother gave birth to Angelina, the fourteenth and last Grimké child. The birth of this child gave Sarah a new purpose in life. She was twelve years old at the time and was old enough to assume much of the care for the new baby.

The practice of an older sister watching over her younger sibling or siblings was not unusual in large families of the nineteenth century. In many families, older sisters were "mothers" to their younger brothers and sisters. The situation most often resulted because of the great demands placed on the mothers of that day, and Mary was no exception. She held responsibility for running a large, complex household, a task that did not leave her with the time or the energy to care for an infant.[14] Her withdrawal from the

---

[12]Sarah Grimké, "The Education of Women," *Letters on the Equality of the Sexes and Other Essays*, ed. Elizabeth Ann Bartlett (New Haven: Yale University Press, 1988) 114.

[13]Ibid.

[14]Marli F. Weiner, *Mistresses and Slaves: Plantation Women in South Carolina, 1830–1880* (Urbana/Chicago: University of Illinois Press, 1998) 30–31.

daily care of Angelina also could be attributed to the fact that she already had given birth to thirteen children. She had experienced many times over the joys of motherhood and was most likely exhausted or even numbed by the continuing physical and emotional demands on her.[15] A final factor that perhaps contributed to this situation was that she had already lost three of her children, two during infancy. Her reluctance to assume the daily care for Angelina could be attributed to the fear that gripped many women of the nineteenth century—that the child would not survive childhood.[16] Thus, it may have been easier for Mary, as it was for other mothers, to avoid growing emotionally attached to a child until there was certainty that the child was going to live past infancy and childhood.[17]

Whatever the underlying reason for Sarah's assumption of the primary care for Angelina, she willingly accepted and even demanded the task. She was not satisfied, however, with merely acting as Angelina's unofficial caretaker. Soon after Angelina's birth, Sarah begged her parents to name her godmother of their youngest daughter. The request was an unusual one for a twelve-year-old girl to make, and her parents did not take Sarah's request seriously. Her sincerity and persistence, however, soon changed their minds.[18]

On the day of Angelina's baptism, Sarah stood beside her parents and promised to cherish, to protect, and to provide training for her "goddaughter." Following the ceremony, Sarah slipped away and shut herself in her room. In her diary, she recorded the

---

[15]Anne Firor Scott, The Southern Lady: From Pedestal to Politics, 1830–1930 (Chicago: University of Chicago Press, 1970) 31.

[16]Bertram Wyatt-Brown, *Honor and Violence in the Old South* (New York: Oxford University Press, 1986) 70. See also Jane Turner Censer, *North Carolina Planters and Their Children: 1800–1860* (Baton Rouge: Louisiana State University Press, 1984) 28.

[17]Catherine Clinton, *The Plantation Mistress: Woman's World in the Old South* (New York: Pantheon Books, 1982) 156–59.

[18]Perry, *Lift Up Thy Voice*, 27.

memories of that eventful day: "With tears streaming down my cheeks, I prayed that God would make me worthy of the task I had assumed, and help me guide and direct my precious child. Oh, how good I resolved to be, how careful in all my conduct, that my life might be blessed to her!"[19] Having uttered this prayer, Sarah set out on what would become a lifetime commitment to provide care and guidance for Angelina.

From the day of the baptism, Sarah took almost complete charge of Angelina, whom she called "Nina." Sarah catered to Angelina's every need by providing nurture and love as well as advice and training. Because of this arrangement, Angelina looked to Sarah as her mother figure and often called Sarah "Mother."[20] Even after the sisters became adults, Angelina continued to address Sarah as "Mother" in their correspondence. Thus, from the time of Angelina's birth, the sisters formed an affectionate but unusual bond.

For several years, Sarah's commitment to care for Angelina proved satisfying. Yet, as Angelina grew older and required less attention, Sarah looked to other sources to overcome the deep disappointment over being denied both educational and career opportunities. The new outlet for Sarah during her teenage years was her involvement in Charleston's social affairs. Just as she had done in all her previous commitments, Sarah plunged wholeheartedly into the life of a stereotypical Southern belle.

Like other daughters of Charleston's elite families, Sarah attended a girls' school, which emphasized correct female behavior rather than intellectual development.[21] There Sarah received instruction in needlework, white on white, stitchery, cross stitch, and perhaps even beadwork. Her teachers introduced her to French, art, and music but did not give her enough training in these areas to master any of them. Most importantly, Sarah received instruction in

---

[19]Sarah Grimké, diary, quoted in Birney, *Sarah and Angelina Grimké*, 13.

[20]Ibid.

[21]Scott, *Lift Up Thy Voice*, 7.

the proper etiquette for a person in her social position. She learned how to "formulate the required witty turn of speech for polite conversation and graceful toasts" and generally how to behave in polite company.[22] Her education consisted of "a little of everything and not very much of anything designed not to tax excessively the gentle female mind."[23]

Apart from the time Sarah spent learning the fine art of being a Southern gentlewoman, she occupied herself by taking part in the social circuit of her day. She made extended visits to the plantations of her cousins and friends and attended balls, teas, and dinner parties given by the finest families in Charleston. Sarah also enjoyed the leisurely activities of horseback riding and picnicking with the other young people of the community.[24]

Judge Grimké, a man of prudence and frugality, did not allow Sarah to devote herself completely to frivolous activities. He sought to instill in her and his other children an appreciation for hard work and practical knowledge, and he continually encouraged them to "never lose an opportunity of learning what is useful. If you never need the knowledge, it will be no burden to have it; and if you should you will be thankful to have it."[25] As a result, Sarah learned to spin and weave, to shell corn, and to pick cotton.

Despite her busy schedule, none of the available educational opportunities, social activities, or physical labor filled the emptiness Sarah felt as a result of being denied the study of law. All attempts to overcome her emptiness, in fact, led her to despise herself and those around her. She questioned her purpose in life and pondered the needless waste of her talents. Yet, with apparently no possibility of breaking out of the traditional role for women in her day, she turned to frivolous activities as a means of occupying her time. At

---

[22]Koch, "The Significance of the Grimké Family," 74.

[23]Gerda Lerner, *The Grimké Sisters from South Carolina: Pioneers for Woman's Rights and Abolition,* Studies in the Life of Women, ed. Gerda Lerner (New York: Schocken Books, 1971) 17.

[24]Ibid., 30–31.

[25]Grimké, diary, quoted in Birney, *Sarah and Angelina Grimké*, 9.

one point, she became so desperate to break away from her feelings of entrapment that she considered an unsuitable marriage.[26] Later in life, she expressed her dismay with this period of her life: "I cannot even now look back to those wasted years without a blush of shame at this prostitution of my womanhood, without a feeling of agony at this utter perversion of the ends of my being."[27] The despair Sarah experienced as a result of being denied her dreams, however, was not the sole cause of her discontent. From her early childhood on, she was deeply disturbed by the treatment received by the slaves on her father's plantation.

When Sarah was four years old, she stumbled upon a slave woman being whipped severely. She was so frightened by the scene that she ran from her home down to the wharf. Half an hour later, Sarah's nurse found her begging a sea captain to take her away to a place where such violence did not occur. Thus, from an early age, Sarah demonstrated sensitivity toward slaves and the treatment they received. Her reaction, however, was not an unusual one for a young Southern child. Young children, whether from the South or the North, were generally frightened when confronted by such violence and cruelty.

Most Southern children in the early nineteenth century eventually overcame their loathing of violence against slaves. Southern children learned early in life to accept slavery and the mistreatment of slaves as part of their way of life, and most children even adopted the their parents' rationalizations that sometimes harsh punishment of slaves was necessary in order to keep them in line.[28] Sarah, however, differed from most Southern children in that she continued throughout her childhood to voice serious misgivings about the institution of slavery.

---

[26]Apparently, Thomas talked Sarah out of accepting a marriage proposal from an unidentified suitor when she was nineteen years old. See Judith Nies, *Seven Women: Portraits from the American Radical Tradition* (New York: Viking Press, 1977) 15.

[27]Grimké, "The Education of Women," 114–15.

[28]Lerner, *The Grimké Sisters from South Carolina*, 19–20.

At some point following the whipping incident, Sarah's father gave her a young slave girl to be her servant and companion. Sarah treated the girl as an equal, sharing all her privileges with the slave. They became inseparable playmates, and when the slave girl died a few years later, Sarah was inconsolable. She refused to accept a new slave, a refusal that baffled her parents, who neither understood nor approved of their daughter's attachment to a mere slave. This lost best friend was the only slave Sarah ever owned.[29]

Sarah's abhorrence of slavery resulted not only from her disgust over the abuse slaves received but also because of the opportunities they were denied. She especially could not understand why slaves were not allowed to learn to read or write. Each Sunday afternoon during her teenage years, Sarah taught Bible classes to the slave children.[30] The children themselves were not permitted to read the Bible, but they were allowed to hear it read and to have Bible lessons taught to them. The prohibition against teaching slaves to read stemmed from the slave-owners' fear that the slaves might read insurrectionary or revolutionary ideas into the Bible.[31] So entrenched was their fear that it had been incorporated into South Carolina law. Teaching a slave to read or write was a crime punishable by a fine of one hundred pounds.[32]

---

[29]Ibid., 20.

[30]Perry, *Lift Up Thy Voice*, 22.

[31]Frank G. Kirkpatrick, "From Shackles to Liberation: Religion, the Grimké Sisters and Dissent," in *Women, Religion, and Social Change,* ed. Yvonne Yazbeck and Ellison Banks Findly (Albany: State University of New York Press, 1985) 435.

[32]George M. Stroud, *A Sketch of the Laws Relating to Slavery in the Several States of the United States of America* (printed by the author, 1856; reprint, New York: Negro Universities Press, 1968) 60. The law was enacted in 1740 and read: "Whereas the having of slaves taught to write, or suffering them to be employed in writing, may be attended with great inconveniences, Be it enacted, That all and every person and persons whatsoever who shall hereafter teach or cause any slave or slaves to be taught to write, or shall use or employ any slave as a scribe in any manner

Sarah, however, saw only the eagerness and the capabilities of these children, and she refused to be constrained by what she deemed to be an unreasonable law. Thus, despite the legal and social ramifications of breaking this law, she secretly gave lessons to a slave girl. Each night while the slave girl was supposed to have been combing and brushing Sarah's hair, Sarah was teaching her to read and write. The two girls worked diligently to conceal their activity. Sarah later revealed that each night "the light was put out, the keyhole screened, and flat on our stomachs, before the fire, with the spelling-book under our eyes, we defied the laws of South Carolina."[33] From this defiance of both law and tradition, Sarah received an almost malicious satisfaction. Her defiance, however, eventually came to the attention of her father, who threatened the slave girl with a whipping and sternly lectured Sarah in the dangers of her actions. Both girls escaped severe punishment. Yet for Sarah, the incident most likely served as a reminder that slaves were in the same position as herself in that they too were denied opportunities to learn.

As a result of her early frustration with the institution of slavery, Sarah rejected many of the typical childhood diversions and instead spent an increasing amount of time riding her horse. Such an attachment to an animal was common among Southern children, but the reason behind Sarah's attachment to her horse was highly unusual. In a letter to a friend written later in her life, Sarah revealed that she enjoyed her daily horseback ride so much because the horse, Hiram, was "a gentle, spirited beautiful creature" who "was neither a slave nor a slave owner."[34] While riding Hiram, she was freed from the presence and pressures of slavery. Such freedom allowed Sarah to leave behind the ugliness and cruelty she associated with that institution.

---

of writing hereafter taught to write, every such person or persons shall for every such offence forfeit the sum of one hundred pounds current money."

[33] Grimké, diary, quoted in Birney, *Sarah and Angelina Grimké*, 12.

[34] Ibid., 11.

Sarah's accounts of her childhood disgust with slavery demonstrate an early sensitivity toward the injustice of the institution and a growing empathy with slaves. Yet, for the most part, her accounts were recorded when she was over the age of thirty and already a committed abolitionist. One must raise the question of whether these memories of strong antislavery feelings during her childhood were in actuality antislavery feelings or whether they were arrived at later as a ready-made explanation for the general feelings of discontent she experienced as a child.[35]

Whether Sarah's childhood frustration was due to an early developed disgust with the institution of slavery or to the denial of her educational and career aspirations, the fact remains that her early years were unhappy and confusing ones. All attempts to find self-fulfillment seemed only to frustrate her more. Even her relationship with her younger sister Angelina proved only to be a brief diversion from her inner turmoil. In her late teen years, Sarah, still seeking a release from her anguish, turned to religion.

Religion had always been a part of Sarah's life. Every Sunday since her birth, she attended worship services at St. Philip's Episcopal Church. The entire family as well as the family's slaves were all expected to be present at these services. The Grimké family's religion, however, extended past these weekly formal worship times. Each day the household, under the direction of Mary Grimké, gathered for morning prayers and Bible readings.[36]

Sarah faithfully participated in all of these religious exercises. She listened to the sermons on the necessity of surrendering to Christ and the danger of delaying one's conversion experience. She participated in the family prayer times and was "scrupulously exact in her private devotion."[37] Yet for her these pious actions were mechanical, a matter of habit rather than of conviction, and "her heart was never touched, her soul never stirred."[38] Sarah was greatly

---

[35]Lerner, *The Grimké Sisters from South Carolina*, 21.

[36]Ibid., 52.

[37]Birney, *Sarah and Angelina Grimké*, 19.

[38]Grimké, diary, quoted in Birney, *Sarah and Angelina Grimké*, 19.

troubled by her inability to experience what she perceived to be a genuine conversion. She worried about her lack of commitment to Christ and her insensitivity to her own need for salvation.

In 1813, Sarah's doubts and fears were relieved for a time when she made the first of several responses to the evangelical appeal. Her initial conversion experience came in the midst of a widespread religious revival. From 1800 on, revivalism had a strong influence throughout the Southern states. The movement was especially prevalent in Southwestern states, such as Kentucky, where protracted revivals or camp meetings found their first expression.[39] Evangelicalism, however, was advancing rapidly everywhere in the South without regard to social standing or denominational affiliation. Poor farm families, middle-class townspeople, and wealthy slave-owners were influenced by the outbreak of revival. Methodists, Presbyterians, Baptists, Congregationalists, Lutherans, and Episcopalians were touched by the religious enthusiasm.[40] There was remarkable cooperation among the various denominations. Doctrinal differences were overlooked with the hopes that more souls would be saved, and many were converted during the revivals.[41] The sermons during the revival period emphasized that sinners should confess their sins to God, discontinue their evil practices, and dedicate themselves to leading useful lives.[42] Thus, conversion meant a renunciation of certain worldly pleasures such as dancing, card playing, and taking trips to the theater. It was under these conditions that Sarah, her mother, and her sister Angelina had evangelical conversion experiences.

---

[39]Mark Noll, *A History of Christianity in the United States and Canada* (Grand Rapids: William B. Eerdmans Publishing Company, 1992) 167.

[40]William Warren Sweet, *Revivalism in America: Its Origin, Growth, and Decline* (New York: Charles Scribner's Sons, 1944) 126–27.

[41]Clement Eaton, *The Civilization of the Old South: The Writings of Clement Eaton*, ed. Albert D. Kirwan (Lexington: University of Kentucky Press, 1968) 184.

[42]Perry, *Lift Up Thy Voice*, 60.

Sarah's first significant religious experience was due in part to the preaching of a Presbyterian minister from Savannah, Georgia: the Reverend Henry Kolloch. In 1813, when she was twenty-one years old, Sarah accompanied an elderly friend to a church service at the local Charleston Presbyterian Church, and at this service she heard the visiting Reverend Kolloch preach. The sermon so impressed Sarah that thirteen years later when recording the event in her diary, she still remembered the text from which he preached and details from his sermon. She wrote, "He described in his own touching, exquisite, powerful language the character of Christ, his tenderness, his yearning compassion, his surpassing love."[43] Sarah was moved by the sermon and believed that she finally had experienced true conversion. Years later she recorded: "My whole being was taken captive. I made a full and free surrender and vowed eternal fealty to Jesus. To manifest my sincerity, in my zeal I burnt my paintings, destroyed my little library of poetry and fiction and gave to the flames my gay apparel."[44] Conversion for Sarah also meant giving up novels, dancing, parties, and picnics and substituting them with religious books, prayer meetings, and visits to the poor and sick. Yet even the stirring words of the Reverend Kolloch did not put to rest Sarah's ambivalent feelings toward religion and conversion. Perhaps her ambivalence suggests that Sarah had enough insight and self-awareness to recognize that conversionist religion did not offer her the appropriate resolution to her spiritual quest.[45]

The depth of her commitment to leave behind what she called "vanity and folly" was soon tested, and she gave in to the desire to return to her former lifestyle.[46] A year later, Sarah once again went to hear Reverend Kolloch, who had returned to Charleston to preach at the Presbyterian Church. Upon hearing his sermon, she felt the

---

[43]Grimké, "The Education of Women," 115.
[44]Ibid.
[45]Perry, *Lift Up Thy Voice*, 32–33.
[46]Ibid.

"arrows of conscience," but she chose to ignore Kolloch's call to faithful commitment to Christ.[47]

Sarah's increasing disregard for evangelical religion continued as she immersed herself completely in the social activities of the winter season. In her diary, she revealed her fascination with "worldly pleasures" during this stage of her life. She wrote: "In the winter of 1813 I was led in an unusual degree into scenes of dissipation and folly. It seemed as if my cup of worldly pleasures was filled to overflowing, and after enjoying all the city afforded, I retired into the country in the Spring with a wealthy and fashionable acquaintance, designing to finish my career of folly."[48]

Sarah was not able to ignore her religious convictions because she once again encountered Reverend Kolloch. Kolloch by now was very much interested in Sarah's spiritual welfare. He drew her into long conversations and warned her of the horrible consequences that would befall her if she persisted in her present course of conduct. His admonitions had a sobering effect on her "butterfly" lifestyle. Her continued reluctance to abandon the lifestyle she had chosen may be attributed to the pressure she received from her friends, who encouraged her to ignore the advice of Kolloch and to continue to enjoy the pleasures of Charleston's fashionable society. Yet Sarah was deeply disturbed by Kolloch's persistent probing questions. In the end, she resigned herself to evangelical Christianity and to give up all "vain and sinful pleasures," but she found no joy in that

---

[47]Sarah Grimké, diary, 3 June 1827, 3, Weld-Grimké Collection, William L. Clements Library, University of Michigan, Ann Arbor. The Clements Library owns six diaries of Sarah. The first diary is dated 19 August 1821–25 April 1824; the second is dated 1 January 1825–30 June 1827; the third is dated 1 July 1827–11 November 1828; the fourth is dated 14 November 1828–15 June 1831; the fifth is dated 19 June 1831–17 September 1833; and the sixth is dated 1 January–3 August 1836. Also in the Clements Library is Sarah's "Account of Religious Development," dated 3 June 1827 and "A Statement of Religious Feelings," dated 14 November 1828. The page numbers listed reflect the numbering in each Grimké diary.

[48]Grimké, diary, 3 June 1827, 3.

decision. Instead, she felt "laden with iniquity and transgression."[49] To overcome these feelings of uncertainly and fear, Sarah immersed herself in doing good works. She fed the hungry, clothed the naked, visited the sick and afflicted, and "vainly hoped these outside works would purify a heart defiled with the pride of life, still the seat of carnal propensities and of evil passions."[50] Her attempt at finding joy and salvation by doing good works, however, failed Sarah as well. In an account of her religious experience, she recorded these words:

> Though I often watered my couch with my tears, and with strong supplications pleaded with my Maker, yet I knew nothing of the sanctifying influence of his holy spirit, and not finding that happiness in religion I anticipated, I, by degrees, through the persuasion of some and the inclination of my depraved heart, began to go a little more into society, and to resume my former manner of dressing, though in much moderation when compared with my former stile.[51]

Sarah's return to her former frivolous lifestyle was once again interrupted by a confrontation with Reverend Kolloch. His rebuke of her conduct, however, seemed only to confuse her more so that she "lost nearly all spiritual sense."[52]

At this point, the lowest in Sarah's spiritual struggle, "the merciful interposition of Providence" intervened.[53] This "merciful interposition of Providence" was none other than the serious decline in her father's health. Judge Grimké's illness, she believed, was a sign from God. Her perception of herself as a backslider and a sinner led her to blame herself for her father's illness. Only true repentance, prayer, and a total devotion to her father, she believed,

---

[49]Ibid., 6.
[50]Ibid., 7.
[51]Ibid., 8.
[52]Ibid., 9.
[53]Ibid.

could bring about her salvation.[54] Indeed, she concluded that only her genuine conversion could save her father from certain death.

When Judge Grimké became ill with a disease that no one in Charleston could diagnose, he decided to go to Philadelphia to consult with a well-known Quaker specialist, Dr. Phillip Synge Physick.[55] Sarah, twenty-six years old at the time, accompanied her father to Philadelphia. Her presence on the trip came at the request of her father, who refused to allow his wife, sons, or even servants to attend him on his journey. Instead, he chose Sarah to be with him on what he knew would be for him an arduous and perhaps final journey.

The extraordinary decision to travel away from his home when he was so gravely ill and to take only his unmarried daughter with him offers insight into the relationship between Judge Grimké and Sarah. Perhaps Grimké, recognizing that death was imminent, did not want to be burdened by having to put up the brave front that was required of a powerful patriarch. Thus, he left behind his wife, sons, and servants and took his favorite daughter Sarah, with whom a mask of courageousness and strength would not be required.[56] Grimké's choice of Sarah may have been an expression of confidence in her, "a belated recognition that of all his children she was the only one whose strength and love he could trust to sustain him through the ordeal."[57] Whatever his reason for requesting Sarah's presence, his choice proved to be a wise one. On the journey, Sarah and her father developed a closeness that offered to both a sustaining power at the time of death.

The Grimkés left Charleston on 15 April 1819, and sailed to Philadelphia, arriving one week later. They remained there for two months while the Judge received treatment from Dr. Physick. During their days in the city, Sarah spent her time seeking to meet

---

[54]Gerda Lerner, *The Feminist Thought of Sarah Grimké* (New York/Oxford: Oxford University Press, 1998) 7.

[55]The exact nature of Judge Grimké's illness is undetermined.

[56]Nies, *Seven Women*, 13.

[57]Lerner, *The Grimké Sisters from South Carolina*, 46.

her father's every need. Her father was just as considerate of Sarah's physical and emotional well-being.

Sarah recorded her memories in her diary of this special yet painful time with her father. Of her new found relationship with her father, she wrote:

> He saw and felt blessed by my efforts even when unsuccessful and sometimes insisted upon my leaving him to walk or ride lest my health should suffer from confinement. Thus, we lived in the constant sacrifice of selfishness to promote each other's gratification and though we loved each other before we became more closely united in the bonds of love which unite a Parent to a child [and those bonds] were more strongly knit and we became Friends indeed. I may say that our attachment became strengthened day by day and that ere our final separation by death we loved each other with the fervent affection which arises from genuine love and unlimited confidence. I regard this as the greatest blessing next to my conversion that I have ever received from God and I think if all my future life is passed in affection this mercy alone should make me willingly yea cheerfully and joyfully to submit myself to the chastisement of the Lord.[58]

This closeness that developed between Sarah and her father was, in her mind, tied to her religious conversion. Sarah had experienced overwhelming guilt as a result of her spiritual struggle and then blamed herself for her father's illness, but as she cared for him and nursed him, she found relief from that guilt.[59] Her selfless care-giving "was the vehicle for finding redemption and inner peace."[60]

---

[58]Grimké, diary, August 1819, 1–2. Sarah wrote this material in 1819 and copied it on 9 January 1821 into her father's diary.

[59]Lerner, *The Feminist Thought of Sarah Grimké*, 7.

[60]Ibid., 8.

The closeness between Sarah and her father continued as they, on the advice of Dr. Physick, traveled to Bordertown, New Jersey, in mid-June. Bordertown was a coastal town and provided "sea-bathing," which the doctor thought would be beneficial to the Judge's health. For a time, this exercise seemed "to revive his drooping spirits and give to his declining health reanimation," and Sarah felt as if they were at "the waters of Bethesda."[61]

On 4 July, the Grimkés journeyed on to Long Branch, another small costal town in New Jersey. The trip itself proved to be almost too much for the ailing Judge, but Sarah hoped that her father's increasingly declining health was merely fatigue and that he would overcome it after a few days of rest. His suffering and pain, however, finally convinced her that her father was indeed close to death. At this point in their journey, Sarah's faith was her sustaining force. She wrote:

> This sudden and unexpected trial almost delivered me of self-possession yet let me here acknowledge of that Almighty Being whose everlasting arms supported me in this hour of severest suffering. I did not mourn or even wish that if it was his will that I should drink the cup even to the dregs it should pass from me, though friendless and alone in a tavern without one human being to soothe or support me I felt a perfect resignation and an assurance that He in whom I trusted would never leave me nor forsake me and that whatever service was appointed me my strength would be sufficient even to the performance of the last sad duties.[62]

As her father's suffering continued, Sarah stayed constantly by his bedside, straining to hear his shallow breathing.

---

[61]Ibid., 2. Sarah makes reference to the New Testament passage in which the blind and lame gathered at a pool in Bethesda where they believed they could receive healing. See John 5:1–4.

[62]Ibid., 4.

The following day Grimké was better, and Sarah was overjoyed. His recovery did not last. The next day was one of anguish. The pattern of days of severe pain and suffering followed by revived health continued for almost a month. All during these days, Sarah provided physical, emotional, and spiritual comfort for her father. She prayed with him and read scripture to him. Despite her loving care, Grimké never gained complete relief from his suffering, but he never complained about his ill health. Instead, as he told her one morning, he accepted his illness and the certainty of his death with calm assurance that his fate was in "the hands of an Almighty Friend, of a merciful Redeemer who does not willingly grieve or affect the children of men and doubtless his everlasting arms are under us."[63] These words were the first ones he had ever spoken to Sarah of his certain death, and he never again broached the subject until a few hours before his death.

On 6 August, Grimké grew visibly worse. Though often incoherent, he managed to express his gratefulness to Sarah for the comfort she provided and to ask that God's blessing be bestowed upon her. For the next two days, he was in great agony at times, yet he never complained. Sarah wrote, "His patience was perfect and his heavenly tranquility unbroken. Sometimes he asked for mercy and once he said with strong confidence, 'Though I walk thro the valley of the shadow of death thy rod and thy staff shall comfort me.'"[64] About eight o'clock on the evening of 8 August 1819, Judge Grimké died in Sarah's arms. She spent the rest of that night alone, very much aware of the presence of her "gracious Redeemer" and thankful that God had at last released her beloved parent from his suffering.

This twenty-six year old woman, who had never been outside the state of South Carolina, now had to arrange for the funeral of her beloved father. He was buried in a little churchyard behind an old Methodist church in Long Branch. The funeral procession was a

---

[63]Ibid., 5.
[64]Ibid., 6.

small one with Sarah, as the only mourner present, walking alone behind the plain wooden coffin. The grave-side service was brief and solemn, and the officiating minister was not even of the Episcopal faith. Thus, a distinguished political leader from South Carolina was laid to rest without any of the traditional pomp and circumstance befitting a man of his station in life. There were no well-dressed pallbearers to carry a handsomely ornamented coffin; no grieving wife or children heavily veiled in mourning attire along with other relatives, neighbors, and slaves to follow along in the funeral procession; no funeral feast lasting for days; and no brilliant funeral oration offered on the Sunday following the burial by a minister who had known Grimké all his life.[65] Instead, John Faucheraud Grimké was buried with only his devoted daughter Sarah present.

Following her father's funeral, Sarah returned to Philadelphia where she stayed for two months in a Quaker family's boarding house. The calmness of her new surroundings as well as the absence of slaves and the simplicity of the Quaker lifestyle had a soothing effect on Sarah during her days of deepest anguish. Her plans for returning to Charleston, however, were finally completed, and she set sail for home in November.

On board ship, Sarah encountered another group of Quakers that included the Morris family. Israel Morris, a successful broker and commission merchant from a prestigious Philadelphia family, was traveling with his wife and eight children. A devout Quaker, Morris engaged Sarah in several long discussions about religion during the voyage. Upon their arrival at the Charleston port, Morris presented Sarah with a copy of John Woolman's journal and gained a promise from her to continue their discussion by mail.[66]

After six months in the North, Sarah's return to her family and home was traumatic. She found that her world changed. Sarah had sent word of her father's death, and with the master of the plantation

---

[65]Lerner, *The Grimké Sisters from South Carolina*, 47.
[66]Ibid., 51.

gone, the family was in mourning, and the management of the household was in disarray. The confusion over the settlement of Judge Grimké's estate, the preoccupation of the older Grimké sons with their own careers and families, and the remoteness of her mother left Sarah in a state of bewilderment.[67]

After the intense demands of the previous six months, Sarah sought comfort from those who had been closest to her. Her family, however, did not provide the consolation she so desperately needed. They were not indifferent to her needs, yet they had neither the time to console her nor an understanding of the distress she was experiencing. They were confused by the young woman who had just returned from burying their husband and father. She was no longer the person they had known. Sarah was indeed different, and she was deeply troubled. She recorded her distress in her diary:

> With Job I dared to curse the day of my birth and to wish I had never seen the light. One day I ventured to quote the passage to my mother. She was greatly shocked, and reproved me seriously. I craved a hiding place in the grave as a rest from the turbulence and distress of my feelings, thinking that no estate could be worse than the present. Sometimes, being unable to pray, unable to command one feeling of good, either natural or spiritual, I was tempted to commit some great crime, thinking I could repent and thus restore my lost sensibility.[68]

The time in the North spent nursing her father and presiding at his death and burial certainly took its toll on Sarah's emotional and spiritual health. Yet, in many ways, the experience was also a liberating one for her.

Judge Grimké's decision to take Sarah along on his journey gave her an opportunity to travel, to see new places, to meet diverse

---

[67]Perry, *Lift Up Thy Voice*, 48.
[68]Grimké, diary, 3 June 1827, 13.

types of people, and to be introduced to varying points of view. The trip also presented her with the chance to be independent. First in Philadelphia and then in the small New Jersey towns, Sarah was the one who made travel plans, contacted physicians, arranged for lodging and meals, and eventually organized a funeral service. She met each challenge the journey presented with confidence and grace and proved herself to be dependable and capable of handling responsibility. Thus, in death as he had never done in life, her father set Sarah free from the confines of traditional southern womanhood.

Now, upon her return to her family and home, Sarah found that she would have to yield her new freedoms and independence in order to gain the approval of her family and community. Not only would she once again have to submit to the confining expectations for Southern women that she now felt were unacceptable; she also would have to live with the daily encounters with the institution of slavery. During her time away from the South, her antipathy toward slavery escalated, and upon her return, she found it increasingly difficult to suppress her disgust and anger. She expressed her feelings in these words:

> From early childhood I had been tried with the condition of the slaves, and had long believed their bondage inconsistent with justice and humanity. After being for many months in Penn[sylvania] when I went back, it seemed as if the sight of their condition was insupportable. It burst on my mind with renewed horror, and I can compare my feeling only with a canker incessantly gnawing—deprived of ability to modify the situation. I was as one in bonds looking on their sufferings [which] I could not soothe or lessen.... Events had made this world look like a wilderness. I saw nothing in it but desolation and suffering.[69]

---

[69]Ibid., 11–12.

Sarah's sadness continued for some months until, in desperation, her mother insisted that she visit relatives in North Carolina, hoping that the change in climate and environment would provide emotional and spiritual healing.

Sarah spent the autumn months of 1820 at a plantation on the Cape Fear River that belonged to her aunt and uncle, James and Marianna Smith. The Smiths warmly welcomed Sarah and provided an atmosphere in which she was free to come to terms with her sadness. Convinced that the cause of her problems was a spiritual one, Sarah spent much of her time attending the services of a small Methodist church near the plantation. Her association with its members finally enabled her to overcome her sadness and apathy. Encouraged by their worship and fellowship and intent upon joining them, she set out to examine their doctrine and practices. Sarah, however, was disappointed with their teachings and found the Methodist church to be just as deficient as the Episcopal church.

The exploration of and dissatisfaction with Methodist doctrine spurred Sarah on to survey all other denominations and sects and to find the one in which she would feel truly comfortable. In her investigation, her only stipulation was that she would become "anything but a Quaker or a Catholic."[70] Despite such a determination, she began to read the journal of John Woolman that Isaac Morris had given to her.

Fascinated by the similarity of Woolman's spiritual pilgrimage to her own, Sarah read and reread the journal. She read the account of his own early inclination toward a frivolous lifestyle and of his guilt and despair over not following the ways of God. Of his struggle, Woolman recorded: "Having attained the Age of sixteen Years, I began to love wanton Company; and though I was preserved from prophane [*sic*] Language, or scandalous Conduct, still I perceived a Plant in me which produced much wild Grapes; yet my merciful Father forsook me not utterly, but, at Times, through his Grace, I was brought seriously to consider my Ways;

---

[70]Ibid., 14.

and the Sight of my Backslidings affected me with Sorrow.[71] Sarah also read of Woolman's growing discomfort and even contempt toward the institution of slavery. He referred to slavery as a "Gloom over the Land" and as a burden that would grow heavier on the shoulders of slave-owners.[72] Sarah could see that Quakerism offered "a resting-place for her weary, sore-travailed spirit."[73] It would seem that Sarah was shifting her attention from conversionist religion to ethical reform. This shift eventually would lead to her abandonment of evangelical religion and to her adoption of Quakerism.

---

[71]John Woolman, *The Journal with Other Writings of John Woolman* (London: J.M. Dent and Sons, n.d.) 19.

[72]Ibid., 32–33.

[73]Birney, *Sarah and Angelina Grimké*, 30.

Chapter 3

Quakerism
Sarah Grimké's Search for Justice
for Slaves and Women

The Religious Society of Friends originated during the seventeenth century and was among several movements that arose in England as a protest to the dominant religious culture of the day. The movement began in 1647 when its founder, George Fox, had a transforming religious experience. Fox immediately started to preach, proclaiming that God could be found within each individual and that religious possibilities reside in all persons regardless of class, race, or nationality.[1] Fox's preaching soon attracted followers, and although the establishment of a new religious sect had not been part of his plan, by 1650 converts to his teachings formed communities and called themselves "Children of Light" and later "Friends in the Truth." Eventually, the sect adopted as its official name "Society of Friends."

The name "Quaker" was not associated originally with Fox's followers but with a sect of women in England who shivered and

---

[1]Elbert Russell, *The History of Quakerism* (New York: Macmillan Company, 1942) 24.

shook during religious experiences.[2] In 1650, Fox and the members
of his sect first were called "Quakers." This reference resulted from
Fox's exhortation to Justice Gervase Bennett that the judge should
tremble at the name of the Lord. This encounter with Bennett and
the fact that Fox's followers were known to tremble and to shake
when under the power of God led the "Children of Light" to acquire
the scornful epithet of "Quakers."

From 1651 to 1654, Fox traveled throughout northern England
preaching his message and winning converts. His unorthodox
teaching often landed him in jail. Yet, despite confrontations with
the authorities, Quakerism established its organization, theology,
and practices within the first years of the movement.

The foremost doctrine that set the Quakers apart from other
religious organizations was their belief in the Inner Light. From the
time of Fox, Quakers believed that the divine light of Christ
enlightened every person; that is, each person received the direct
revelation of Christ. The Inner Light led individuals gradually into
salvation. Quaker religious life consequently focused on spiritual
growth or regeneration rather than on a singular salvation
experience.[3]

As a result of the Quaker emphasis on the indwelling of
individuals by the Inner Light, all intermediaries—such as priests,
sacraments, and creeds—between humanity and God were deemed
unnecessary and rejected. Even scripture became secondary to the
authority of the Inner Light.[4] The doctrine of the Inner Light,
therefore, directly influenced Quaker beliefs about the equality of all
persons. Because everyone—regardless of culture, nationality, race,
or gender—could receive the Light, Quakers reasoned that all

---

[2]William C. Braithwaite, *The Beginnings of Quakerism*, 2d ed. rev. by
Henry J. Cadbury (Cambridge: University Press, 1955) 57.

[3]John Punshon, *Portrait in Grey: A Short History of the Quakers*
(London: Quaker Home Service, 1984) 48–49.

[4]Wilmer A. Cooper, *A Living Faith: An Historical and Comparative
Study of Quaker Beliefs*, 2d ed. (Richmond IN: Friends United Press, 2001)
27–30.

persons must be morally equal. As a result, the early Quaker meetings welcomed the participation of women in worship and as ministers.[5]

Fox's willingness to defend the rights of women established early on the Society of Friends' position on women. He believed that women should have an integral place in the church. The participation of women, he said, must not be restricted. Women should be allowed to serve in any capacity including the role of minister. If the Holy Spirit is accessible to all persons, Fox reasoned, no one has the right to interfere with the Spirit's work on the basis of gender. In expressing his view on women ministers, he wrote, "You that persecute the daughters, on whom the spirit of the Lord is poured, and believe them not, you are they that despise the prophets, and despise prophesying, and so have broken the apostles' command."[6] He continued in his support for women ministers by writing: "So be ashamed forever, and let all your mouths be stopped forever, that despise the spirit of prophecy in the daughters, and do cast them into prison, and do hinder the women-labourers in the gospel."[7] Fox's respect for and admiration of women and his belief in their full equality before God were instrumental in the Society of Friends' adoption of gender equality.[8] His openness to women serving as ministers also attracted many women, and Quaker membership quickly became predominantly female.

Sixty years after Fox made his views on the equality of the sexes known, the Quaker William Penn wrote, "Sexes made no Difference; since in Souls there is none."[9]

Penn's views on female equality were reflective of the American Quakerism. In the American colonies, Quakers allowed

---

[5]Ibid.

[6]George Fox, *The Works of George Fox, Vol. 4* (New York: Isaac T. Hopper, 1831; reprint, New York: AMS, 1975) 106.

[7]Ibid., 109.

[8]Margaret Hope Bacon, *Mothers of Feminism: The Story of Quaker Women in America* (San Francisco: Harper and Row, 1986) 22.

[9]William Penn, *Fruits of Solitude* (London: Northcott, 1693) 33.

large numbers of women to serve as religious leaders, and they licensed women as "Public Friends" so that they could spread God's word. By 1800, almost half of the Quaker ministers in the Philadelphia Yearly Meeting were women, and dozens of these women served as itinerant ministers both in America and abroad.[10] The writings of Fox and Penn along with the practice of American Quakers revealed that many early Quakers—especially the leaders—emphasized gender equality.[11]

Because of their emphasis on individualism in matters of salvation, Quakers refused to establish a hierarchical system of leadership. They acknowledged, however, that God, through the Inner Light, called out individuals to be ministers. These ministers proclaimed God's message of salvation and provided leadership. A member of the sect became a minister upon the issuance of a "recommendation" by their monthly meeting. The "recommendation" usually was based on the frequency and content of a candidate's extemporaneous utterances made during worship and was a formal recognition that a gift had been bestowed on a person.[12]

Unlike the standard practice of other denominations, Quaker ministers did not receive financial compensation for their services. Quakers considered paid ministers to be "hireling" ministers. Paying ministers was an abomination because it directly contradicted Christ's instructions to his disciples to "freely give" just as they had

---

[10]Catherine A. Brekus, "The Revolution in the Churches: Women's Religious Activism in the Early American Republic," in *Religion and the New Republic: Faith in the Founding of America*, ed. James H. Hutson (Lanham: Rowman & Littlefield Publishers, Inc., 2000) 120.

[11]Phyllis Mack, "Gender and Spirituality in Early English Quakerism," in *Witnesses for Change: Quaker Women over Three Centuries*, ed. Elisabeth Potts Brown and Susan Mosher Stuard (New Brunswick: Rutgers University Press, 1989) 31–57.

[12]Hugh Barbour and J. William Frost, *The Quakers* (New York: Greenwood Press, 1988) 103.

"freely received" (Matt 10:8).[13] Quaker ministers, therefore, were generally lay ministers, most of whom worked in secular positions in order to support themselves and their families.[14] The sect, however, did not reject the use of offerings to provide at least some financial support for ministers when the monies were given freely and voluntarily.[15]

According to the Quakers, the doctrine of the Inner Light made formal education both unnecessary and undesirable.[16] The Society of Friends taught that preaching and other ministries should be inspired by the Holy Spirit. Preparation, therefore, interfered with the work of the Spirit. As a result of their attitude toward education and preparation, Quakers developed an anti-intellectual bias. Such a bias caused the Society of Friends as a whole to fall far behind other denominations in building and populating their institutions of higher education.[17]

---

[13]Braithwaite, *The Beginnings of Quakerism*, 136.

[14]Thomas D. Hamm, *The Transformation of American Quakerism: Orthodox Friends, 1800–1907* (Bloomington/Indianapolis: Indiana University Press, 1988) 8.

[15]Braithwaite, *The Beginnings of Quakerism*, 136.

[16]Punshon, *Portrait in Grey*, 62.

[17]Despite their bias against higher education, the Quakers had provided leadership in the area of primary education for many years. In the 1830s, there seems to have been an increasing interest among Quakers in secondary education. One indication of their interest is that they established eight academies between 1830 and 1860. In the preceding 140 years before 1830, they had established only 8 academies in America. Although only a few Quaker children attended these academies in the early nineteenth century, most Quakers thought the academies necessary or at least desirable. Not until 1850, however, did the Quakers display an interest in higher education, and even then, there seems to have been much skepticism among the Society of Friends members as to the benefits of allowing members to attend such colleges as Oberlin, Amherst, or Harvard. By the end of the nineteenth century, the Society of Friends apparently came to accept the need for higher education and, as a result, established Haverford College and Earlham College. See Hamm, *The Transformation of American Quakerism*, 8, 39–40.

Another distinctive belief that set the Quakers apart was their understanding of Scripture. Because of the primacy of the Inner Light, Quakers tended to minimize the importance of Scripture. Such an understanding does not mean that they rejected it or that they did not hold it in high esteem. Rather, Scripture's significance derived from its being the record of God's historical activity and of Christ's life and death.[18]

For Quakers, however, Scripture was a secondary revelation, while inward illumination by the Holy Spirit was the primary revelation. The Bible, therefore, served as a guidebook that would lead its readers to experience for themselves the truths recorded in it.[19] The Quaker de-emphasis on Scripture resulted in the Bible rarely being read during worship services.[20] The Quaker worship services differed in several other ways from the services of more traditional denominations. Quaker worshipers and ministers sat in silence unless directly inspired by the Holy Spirit to speak. This most prominent distinctive allowed worshipers to block out all distractions and to wait expectantly on the movement of God. The emphasis on silence, however, did not eliminate speaking. Speaking aloud in a Quaker meeting was a serious act, one that required prayerful and thoughtful consideration.[21] Because of the seriousness with which Quakers viewed breaking the silence of worship, few of them ever spoke in the services. Those who did feel prompted to speak, however, apparently did so on a regular basis.[22]

Despite the strong emphasis on individual reception of and response to the Inner Light, Quakerism did not promote pure individualism. Instead, it taught that the highest knowledge of the divine could best be achieved in a corporate setting. The will of God could be known most fully and the Inner Light could be experienced most clearly when believers gathered in worship and together

---

[18]Russell, *The History of Quakerism*, 51–54.

[19]Ibid., 53–54.

[20]Hamm, *The Transformation of American Quakerism*, 8.

[21]Russell, *The History of Quakerism*, 55, 237.

[22]Hamm, *The Transformation of American Quakerism*, 8.

sought spiritual discernment.[23] Thus, corporate worship services constituted a vital role in an individual's religious development.

Although there was no planned structure for a Quaker worship service, the meeting usually began with an extended period of silence, followed by the testimonies of those who felt moved by the Spirit. Quakers who spoke in meetings generally gave their personal spiritual testimony or delivered a lengthy, extemporaneous sermon that was called the "ministry."[24] Little is known about the content of their sermons, at least before 1850, but several themes seem to have dominated their preaching. These themes included the Inner Light, spiritual baptism, spiritual growth, plain living, the importance of silence, and the dangers of the world. The usually biblically based messages were characterized by allegorical and metaphorical language.[25] Eventually, members who regularly preached or spoke in meetings were recognized by their meetings as ministers.

The Quaker doctrine of plainness was another of the sect's distinctive practices. Quakers rigorously enforced a plain lifestyle by insisting on simplicity of dress and speech. Plainness in dress meant wearing only dull colors and avoiding clothes with any unnecessary frills or buttons.[26] They advocated simple and drab fashions as a "hedge and defence [*sic*] " against manners and customs of the world.[27]

Plainness in speech meant refusing to follow the English custom of addressing inferiors as "thee" and "thou" while addressing superiors as "you." Fox and his followers refused to

---

[23]Russell, *The History of Quakerism*, 55.

[24]Punshon, *Portrait in Grey*, 61.

[25]Hamm, *The Transformation of American Quakerism*, 8. See also Melvin B. Endy, Jr. "The Society of Friends," in Vol. 1 *Encyclopedia of the American Religious Experience: Studies of Traditions and Movements*, ed. Charles H. Lippy and Peter Williams (New York: Charles Scribner's Sons, 1988) 600.

[26]Punshon, *Portrait in Grey*, 129.

[27]Rufus Jones, *The Faith and Practice of Quakers* (Richmond IN: Friends United Press, 1980) 99.

adapt their speech in a manner that would differentiate between status or class. They addressed all persons with "thee" and "thou."[28] Quakers also refused to remove their hats for members of the court. Such an act, the Quakers reasoned, did not coincide with their belief in the equality of all persons or with their belief that signs of respect should be reserved solely for God.[29]

Plain living for Quakers meant an avoidance of such "vices" as sports, cards, dice, plays, dancing, intemperate drinking, reading fiction, and listening to instrumental music.[30] These restrictions came as a result of the Quaker belief that any activity that stirred up one's emotions could pose a danger to spiritual development.[31] The restrictions also developed out of the Quaker conviction concerning the proper use of time. Because of the fragility and shortness of life, Quakers reasoned that all activities should reflect one's commitment to God.

In an attempt to keep from becoming entangled with the world, the Quakers ruled that members of their sect should not marry outside the Society of Friends.[32] The rationale behind the rule was that marriage between a Quaker and a non-Quaker would result in spiritual confusion for the children born to that union. The Society of Friends further contended that mixed marriages would interfere with the plain and simple lifestyle adopted by the Quaker partner.[33] The regulations concerning marriage kept the Quaker community tightly intertwined and allowed its members to isolate themselves to a certain extent from the outside world. These regulations also resulted in members of the sect clustering in limited geographic

---

[28]A. Neave Brayshaw, *The Quakers: Their Story and Message* (New York: Macmillan Co., 1938) 125.

[29]Russell, *The History of Quakerism*, 55.

[30]Stow Persons, *American Minds: A History of Ideas*, rev. ed. (Malabar FL: Robert E. Krieger Publishing Co., 1983) 62.

[31]Punshon, *Portrait in Grey*, 132.

[32]Barbour and Frost, *The Quakers*, 112–14.

[33]Hamm, *The Transformation of American Quakerism*, 9.

regions such as eastern Pennsylvania and eastern and southwestern Ohio.[34]

From the earliest days of the Society of Friends, members demonstrated sensitivity to human need and a concern for the welfare of others.[35] Quakers felt deeply about many causes and willingly expended vast amounts of time and energy to bring about needed changes. Those causes included prison reform, education, peace, and suffrage. Commitment to acts of benevolence and humanitarianism, the Quakers believed, indicated outward purity as well as the work of the Inner Light.[36]

The most obvious example of the commitment to humanitarian causes was many Quakers' involvement in the movement to abolish slavery. The concern for persons held in bondage can be traced back to Fox, who voiced his uneasiness about slavery as early as the 1650s.[37] The most fearless and outspoken Quaker opponents of slavery, however, lived in America.

Quakers began migrating to America as early as the 1670s. Their flight from the British Isles stemmed primarily from the persecution they faced there. The first groups of Quakers to arrive settled in West Jersey and Pennsylvania, where they eventually

---

[34]Ibid., 10.

[35]Sydney V. James, *A People Among Peoples: Quaker Benevolence in Eighteenth-Century America* (Cambridge: Harvard University Press, 1963) 25–26.

[36]Hamm, *The Transformation of American Quakerism*, 10.

[37]In 1657, George Fox wrote one of the earliest English discussions of slavery. It came in the form of a letter addressed to Quaker missionaries in the New World, "To Friends Beyond Sea, that Have Blacks and Indian Slaves." In this letter, Fox did not denounce slavery but reminded the missionaries that all persons were equal in the eyes of God. Fourteen years later while visiting Barbados, Fox wrote his first treatise against the practice of slavery. It was titled *To the Ministers, Teachers, and Priests, (So called, and so Stileing your Selves) in Barbadoes.* See Thomas E. Drake, *Quakers and Slavery in America* (New Haven: Yale University Press, 1950) 2–5.

became the ruling elite instead of the embattled minority.[38] The first Quakers in America preoccupied themselves with establishing their communities and their meetings. Not until the late 1680s did they express their concerns about the presence of slavery and the slave trade and begin to articulate an antislavery rhetoric. Yet, when the Quakers did become involved in the issue of slavery, they were "the crucial variable which prompted a few colonial Americans to free their slaves and to begin a campaign which would awaken the world to the injustice built into the peculiar institution."[39]

In their opposition to slavery, Quakers were confronted by the fact that the institution existed in biblical times and that no specific Bible passage prohibited slavery. Without specific biblical evidence, Quakers began to rely on passages such as the Golden Rule (Matt 7:12; Luke 6:31) to cast doubts on the morality of holding another human being in bondage.[40] Yet because they did not hold the Bible to be the ultimate and final revelation of God, Quakers were free to apply their distinctive beliefs to the issue of slavery. Their understanding of the Inner Light and its availability to all persons led them to repudiate the assertion that blacks were unfit to be Christians because of their natural inferiority.[41] Quakers also relied on their unique method of decision-making to reject slavery. They argued that by silently waiting on the Lord, they had been led to believe that slavery was sinful.

In 1688, the Quakers of Germantown, Pennsylvania, issued the first American-published protest against the institution of slavery. The protest—signed by William Southeby, Benjamin Lay, John Woolman, and Anthony Benezet—called for an end to the slave trade and to slavery. The Germantown document stated that slavery was inconsistent with Christianity and that members of the Society

---

[38]Jean R. Soderlund, *Quakers and Slavery: A Divided Spirit* (Princeton: Princeton University Press, 1985) 7.

[39]J. William Frost, Introduction to *The Quaker Origins of Antislavery*, ed. J. William Frost (Norwood PA: Norwood Editions, 1980) 28.

[40]Ibid., 5.

[41]Ibid., 2.

of Friends should refrain from owning slaves.[42] Eight years later, the Philadelphia Yearly Meeting declared that Quakers should discontinue any involvement in the importing and selling of slaves. Owning slaves was not banned outright, but the action taken by the Philadelphia Meeting was an early move toward the eventual Quaker rejection of slavery.[43] The Philadelphia Meeting also encouraged its members to teach any slaves they owned to read, to give them a Christian education, and to release them after a reasonable time of service.[44]

Firmly established by the 1750s, the Philadelphia Yearly Meeting began sending letters and ministers to other yearly meetings throughout the colonies to persuade other Quakers that slavery was a sin. Quakers in New England, New York, North Carolina, Virginia, Maryland, and Pennsylvania all followed the example of the Philadelphia Meeting in denouncing the ownership of slaves.[45] Merely freeing the slaves was not the only concern of Quakers. By the 1750s, the Quakers had addressed racial prejudice, education for former slaves, and aid for fugitive slaves. All of these issues would become central to later discussions among abolitionists.[46]

By 1776, the Philadelphia Yearly Meeting had intensified its fight against slavery by prohibiting its members from owning slaves. The Quakers also came to the logical conclusion that the obligation to liberated slaves did not cease with the act of manumission. Thus, some members formed schools for former slaves, assisted runaway slaves in their escapes, and organized boycotts of goods produced by slave labor.[47] All these early activities eventually led the Society of Friends in 1796 to open its membership to persons of all races.

---

[42]Soderlund, *Quakers and Slavery*, 4.
[43]Drake, *Quakers and Slavery in America*, 20.
[44]Ibid., 18–20.
[45]Frost, *The Quakers*, 12.
[46]Ibid., 24.
[47]Drake, *Quakers and Slavery in America*, 77.

The early protests voiced by the Society of Friends against the slave trade and slaveholding resulted in the Quakers having the greatest antislavery influence of any religious body in colonial America.[48] Such influence enabled the Quakers to lead in organizing abolition societies. In 1775, Pennsylvania Quakers established the "Pennsylvania Society for Promoting the Abolition of Slavery, for the Relief of Free Negroes Unlawfully Held in Bondage, and for Improving the Condition of the African Race." They soon formed similar societies in New York, North Carolina, Rhode Island, New Jersey, Delaware, Maryland, and Connecticut.[49] Quakers also actively participated in the formation of a national antislavery society. Of the sixty-two men and women who met in Philadelphia on 4 December 1833 to organize the American Anti-Slavery Society, twenty-one of them were Quakers.[50]

Quaker involvement in the abolition movement, however, was neither universal nor unanimous. Many persons within the Society of Friends fiercely objected to members joining antislavery organizations. Involvement in abolition societies, they argued, violated the unity and purity of the Quaker meetings.[51] Such a violation occurred because participation in abolition societies meant associating with non-Quakers, who did not wait for the leading of the Holy Spirit and who often were of doubtful religious and moral standing.[52] The Society of Friends also cited the use of political methods to achieve the emancipation of slaves as a second reason

---

[48]William W. Sweet, *The Story of Religion in America* (New York: Harper and Row, 1930; reprint, Grand Rapids: Baker Book House, 1983) 287.

[49]H. Larry Ingle, *Quakers in Conflict: The Hicksite Reformation* (Knoxville: University of Tennessee Press, 1986) 5–6. See also Soderlund, *Quakers and Slavery*, 185.

[50]Louis Filler, *The Crusade Against Slavery, 1830–1860* (New York: Harper and Row, 1960) 66.

[51]Soderlund, *Quakers and Slavery*, 17.

[52]Hamm, *The Transformation of American Quakerism*, 32.

that involvement in the abolition movement was inappropriate for Quakers.

Despite the years of participation in and commitment to societies that were established to eradicate slavery, the politicizing of the abolition movement and the inclusive membership of such societies caused tension within many local Quaker meetings. Some meetings refused to allow antislavery lecturers to speak at their gatherings. Other meetings encouraged or even demanded that its members refrain from being associated with abolition societies. Quakers who ignored the Society of Friends' ban on involvement in the antislavery movement often were disfellowshiped.[53] Thus, it would seem that the Society of Friends placed greater emphasis on the restrictions established by meetings than it did on the appeals of individual members to the leadership of the Inner Light.[54]

The debate within the Society of Friends over involvement in the abolition movement continued during the 1830s and 1840s. Because of the issue of abolition, many Quaker meetings became battlegrounds. Most meetings affirmed the historic Quaker opposition to slavery, but Quakers who refused to conform to the ban on involvement in antislavery organizations faced their meetings' discipline.[55]

In the early years of the nineteenth century, the Society of Friends attracted numerous converts. Many of the converts had experienced social alienation. They were men and women who, because of moral or political reasons, could no longer espouse the views held by their families, friends, or churches. Sarah Grimké was among these converts. No longer comfortable being a Southern gentlewoman and no longer able to overcome her aversion to slavery or the religious teachings of most Southern churches, Sarah turned to Quakerism with the hope that she would find peace and security. The Quaker opposition to slavery and the slave trade, its acceptance of women ministers, and its emphasis on individual

---

[53]Punshon, *Portrait in Grey*, 180.
[54]Hamm, *The Transformation of American Quakerism*, 32.
[55]Ibid., 32–33.

enlightenment drew Sarah to this religious group. Yet her
conversion to Quakerism also may be attributed to the fact that she
was introduced to the tenets of this faith at a vulnerable and
receptive period in her life—the weeks following the death of her
father.

In April 1819, Sarah traveled with her father on a trip to the
North. The trip, prompted by Judge Grimké's failing heath and his
desire for medical treatment, proved to be unsuccessful. Grimké
died in a small New Jersey coastal town on 8 August 1819. After
burying her father, Sarah returned home to Charleston, where she
discovered that she no longer felt comfortable with her family or
with the southern way of life. Her discomfort caused a prolonged
personal crisis for more than a year, a period described in her diary
as a time of inner turmoil, despair, and isolation.[56] Gone was the
freedom from the oppressive and rigid atmosphere of the South that
she experienced during her days in the North. At the lowest point in
her personal crisis, Sarah turned to Quaker writings and to the
friendships she had established with Quakers in hopes that she
might find a sense of comfort or peace. She corresponded faithfully
with Israel Morris, the prominent Quaker she met on her return trip
to Charleston. Morris offered her hope and encouragement,
provided answers for her questions concerning Quakerism, and
readily sent her more Quaker literature.[57]

Sarah also read the journal of John Woolman, whose words
seemed as though they had been written just for her. Woolman
wrote of his spiritual struggles, many that were identical to the
struggles Sarah experienced. He also described his concern for
slaves and his antipathy toward the institution of slavery, concerns
Sarah knew only too well. Yet Woolman's diary revealed that he

---

[56]Sarah Grimké, diary, 15 January 1823, 23–24; 3 June 1827, 11–13,
Weld-Grimké Collection, William L. Clements Library, University of
Michigan, Ann Arbor.

[57]Gerda Lerner, *The Grimké Sisters from South Carolina: Pioneers for
Woman's Rights and Abolition, Studies in the Life of Women,* ed. Gerda
Lerner (New York: Schocken Books, 1971) 54–55.

had found peace despite the internal conflicts he experienced. His peace and security came from Quakerism.[58] Reading Woolman's diary gave Sarah the hope that she too would be able to overcome her inner struggle.

The discovery of an affinity with the writing of John Woolman and the Quakers led Sarah to immerse herself in Quakerism. She faithfully read Quaker literature, including *The Friend*, a weekly newspaper of the Society of Friends.[59] After a few months, Sarah, now twenty-eight years old, attended her first Quaker worship service. The small congregation met in a simple building in Charleston. The silent worship, the absence of adornments and ceremony, and the emphasis on direct, personal communication with God deeply affected Sarah. After attending this Quaker meeting, Sarah knew if she had any affiliation with the Quakers she would be cut off from all persons and institutions that she had cherished from childhood. She knew that she would be ridiculed or even ostracized by her family, friends, and Southern society at large.[60] Thus, despite the warmth and comfort she experienced at the meeting, Sarah was reluctant to convert wholeheartedly to Quakerism. Yet she was experiencing already such a profound loneliness that the prospect of further alienation did not seem to be enough to prevent her from reaching out to what she saw as the only answer to her unhappiness, and she eventually decided to attend the meetings on a regular basis.[61]

During her attendance at the Quaker meetings, Sarah believed that God commanded her to rise and to make a public declaration of

---

[58]John Woolman, *The Journal With Other Writings of John Woolman* (London: J.M. Dent and Sons, n.d.) 32–33.

[59]Elizabeth Ann Bartlett, Introduction to *Letters on the Equality of the Sexes and Other Essays, by Sarah Grimké* (New Haven: Yale University Press, 1988) 16.

[60]Gerda Lerner, *The Feminist Thought of Sarah Grimké* (New York/Oxford: Oxford University Press, 1998) 8.

[61]Sarah Grimké, diary, 3 January 1827, 14–16.

her commitment to do his will.[62] She felt too uncertain and too frightened to obey the command, and she usually left the meetings without speaking to anyone. Sarah soon became convinced, however, that she had experienced not only a divine call to convert to Quakerism but also a call to be a minister. Because of her natural shyness and reticence about speaking before crowds, Sarah responded to her new calling with trepidation.[63] Every meeting became "like a craven" to her. She was repeatedly led by the Spirit to stand and to speak before the congregation, but she resisted these impulses.[64] Her resistance left Sarah feeling guilty about her lack of obedience, and she was certain that she had sinned against the Holy Spirit, that God would never forgive her, and that no sacrifice she could make would ever atone for her disobedience.[65]

Clearly, the peace and reassurance that Sarah hoped to find in Quakerism did not come. Instead, she only found more misery. She continued to correspond with Morris, who encouraged and comforted her. His sympathetic letters led Sarah to conclude that God was commanding her to forsake her home and family and to settle in an area that was more receptive to her new beliefs. Her decision to leave home, Sarah believed, was a response to her religious convictions.[66] That she came to such a conclusion is not surprising given the increasing hostility she experienced as a result of converting to Quakerism. Her family and friends reproached her daily and ridiculed her new religious beliefs. Escaping the hostile atmosphere and achieving some measure of peace could only happen, Sarah realized, if she left Charleston and relocated in a

---

[62]Katharine Du Pre Lumpkin, *The Emancipation of Angelina Grimké* (Chapel Hill: University of North Carolina Press, 1974) 19; and Catherine Birney, *Sarah and Angelina Grimké: The First Women Advocates of Abolition and Woman's Rights* (Westport CT: Greenwood Press, Publishers, 1969) 30.

[63]Sarah Grimké, diary, 1 July 1827, 1.

[64]Ibid., 14 September 1827, 22–23.

[65]Birney, *Sarah and Angelina Grimké*, 31–32.

[66]Ibid., 32.

Northern state. The most natural place for her to go when she left Charleston was Philadelphia, the home of Israel Morris. Morris had encouraged Sarah to leave the South, and he had offered her a home with him and his family.[67] His encouragement and invitation prompted Sarah to action. In spring 1821, she informed her family of her decision to leave home, and she prepared to move to Philadelphia.

Deciding to leave her family and home was a radical step for Sarah. Unmarried Southern women were expected to live quiet lives and to remain in their family home or to live with siblings. They were not to move to a city hundreds of miles away and live among strangers.[68] Sarah, however, was able to break with the expectations of her family and of Southern society because of the money she had inherited upon her father's death. Judge Grimké bequeathed each of his children $10,000, which allowed Sarah a certain freedom that she would not have had otherwise. It ensured that she could sustain a modest level of living apart from her family.[69]

On 15 May 1821, Sarah left Charleston for Philadelphia. To soften the radicalness of her actions, Sarah begged her younger sister, Anna Grimké Frost, to accompany her to Philadelphia. Anna, the widow of an Episcopal minister and the mother of a young daughter, agreed to travel with Sarah and relocate in Philadelphia.[70]

---

[67]Ibid.

[68]Lerner, *The Grimké Sisters from South Carolina*, 57–58.

[69]Birney, *Sarah and Angelina Grimké*, 35. Sarah allowed Isaac Lloyd, a fellow Quaker, to invest her inheritance. The dividends allowed her to remain financially independent throughout the remainder of her life. See Lerner, *The Grimké Sisters from South Carolina*, 254.

[70]Although she was not an opponent of slavery, Anna recognized the detrimental influences that it had on society, and she desired to protect her daughter from such influences. She also was concerned about being able to supplement her inheritance so that she could provide adequately for her daughter. Sarah convinced Anna that she could open a small private school in Philadelphia. Such a venture by a widow of Anna's social status and prestige would not have gained approval in Charleston. See Judith Nies, *Seven Women: Portraits from the American Radical Tradition* (New York:

Anna's decision enabled Sarah to leave Charleston without being
the subject of excessive speculation or gossip. The Grimké family
did not protest the sisters' departure. If the family had realized that
the move was not temporary, perhaps they might have reacted
differently. Yet they were satisfied in believing that Sarah was
merely making the trip for the sake of her health and that she would
return in a few months fully recovered from her fanaticism. In some
ways, Sarah's decision to leave was welcomed by her family.
Despite their love and affection for her, Sarah's new religious
convictions and her somber habits had become a source of tension
and unhappiness in the Grimké home. Thus, they welcomed her
departure simply because it brought an end to the conflict.[71]

Once in Philadelphia, the sisters found lodging for themselves.
Anna and her daughter settled in a boarding house, and Sarah
moved to Greenhill Farm, the home of the Morris family.[72] These
living arrangements seem rather odd in that Sarah chose to live with
virtual strangers instead of her sister. A few months after Sarah
arrived in Philadelphia, Morris's sister Catherine, a devout and strict
Quaker woman, invited Sarah to leave the farm and to live with her
in the city, an arrangement that continued for the fifteen years Sarah
spent in Philadelphia.

During her early years in Philadelphia, Sarah matured
personally, intellectually, and theologically. Her friendship with
Morris assured her of a positive reception by the Society of Friends,
and she began attending the Fourth and Arch Street Meeting. Sarah,
however, hesitated in making formal application for membership in
that group.[73] Only after she had lived in Philadelphia for eighteen
months did Sarah finally seek formal admission into this meeting. In

---

Viking Press, 1977) 15; Larry Ceplair, ed., *The Public Years of Sarah and
Angelina Grimké: Selected Writings, 1835–1839* (New York: Columbia
University Press, 1989) 14; and Lerner, *The Grimké Sisters from South
Carolina*, 97.

[71]Lerner, *The Feminist Thought of Sarah Grimké*, 9.

[72]Sarah Grimké, diary, 15 July 1827, 2.

[73]Ibid., 15 September 1821, 17; 26 October 1821, 19.

February 1823, she submitted her application, and an admissions committee questioned her thoroughly concerning her decision to join the Society.[74] The committee concluded that Sarah needed further instruction in the ways of Quakerism before committing herself to their faith. She finally became a member of the Fourth and Arch Street Meeting on 29 May 1823.[75]

From the time of her admission into the Society of Friends, Sarah was convinced more than ever that she had been called to be a minister. Yet, instead of fulfilling her calling, Sarah sought other forms of service. She taught at charity schools, visited prisons, and attended the monthly, quarterly, and yearly meetings. Despite these worthwhile activities, she became restless and sought something more meaningful to fill her days. As she searched for a vocation that suited her, Sarah's conscience continued to convict her to obey God's call to speak words of admonition to his followers. Yet she still lacked the courage to be obedient. Her diary reveals her constant struggle and her doubts about following God's calling. She wrote: "I was not only guilty of actual disobedience when the call was first presented but continued for several years struggling.... The prevailing feeling of my mind was that it was impossible that I could ever yield myself to this work.... My own will was gradually overcome and then arose the desire that He would strengthen [me] for his service."[76] Sarah's struggle with her calling continued for several years, during which she occasionally summoned the courage to quote Scripture, voice a prayer, or say a few words of encouragement in Quaker meetings.[77]

During Sarah's struggle concerning her call to the Quaker ministry, Catherine Morris, a Quaker Elder, served as Sarah's confidante and advisor. Catherine encouraged Sarah to seek a "recommendation" from the monthly meeting to be a minister and

---

[74]Ibid., 23 March 1823, 33.
[75]Lerner, *The Grimké Sisters from South Carolina*, 59.
[76]Sarah Grimké, diary, 14 September 1827, 23.
[77]Birney, *Sarah and Angelina Grimké*, 38.

assured her that her request would be approved.[78] Sarah, however, felt unqualified for such a position. While she found the thought of speaking before a congregation intriguing, it frightened her. Failure also frightened Sarah. She expressed to Catherine her doubts about her speaking ability and her desire to be nothing less than a brilliant success if she ever stood before a Quaker congregation. Yet, because of the Quaker emphasis that all utterances made at their meetings be spontaneous, Sarah could not prepare herself to speak at their meetings. As a young girl, she always prepared herself for legal debates with her brothers, and now as a thirty-year-old woman, the thought of speaking extemporaneously terrified her. Her uncertainty about her speaking ability and her lack of preparation proved to be disastrous. The few times Sarah spoke at meetings she alternated between speaking too hastily and speaking too hesitantly.[79]

Sarah's poor performance did not impress the members of the Fourth and Arch Street Meeting. Many of them criticized her feeble attempts to speak. Because of her unimpressive and hasty delivery, some Quakers accused her of preparing her statements before the worship service. In her diary, she revealed the depth of her disappointment, especially with the reaction of the Quaker leadership to her attempts at becoming a minister:

> The suffering passed through in meeting, on account of the ministry, feeling as if I were condemned already whenever I arise; the severe reproofs administered by an elder to whom I did a little look for kindness; the cutting charge of preparing what I had to say out of meeting, and going there to preach, instead of to worship…was almost too much for me. It cost me hours of anguish; but Jesus allayed the storm and gave me peace; for in looking at my poor services I can truly say it is not so, although my mind is

---

[78]Lerner, *The Grimké Sisters from South Carolina*, 60.
[79]Birney, *Sarah and Angelina Grimké*, 96.

often brought under exercise on account of this work, and many are the sleepless hours I pass in prayer for preservation in it, feeling it indeed an awful thing to be a channel of communication between God and His people.[80]

The leadership denounced the content of her speeches as well as her method of delivery. Their criticism hurt Sarah deeply, and she interpreted the criticism as a personal condemnation. Although she perhaps was being overly sensitive, there seems to have been justification for Sarah's discouragement. The Quaker leaders clearly were opposed to her ministry. The opposition to Sarah's desire to serve as a minister seems ironic given the traditional Quaker openness to the participation of women. This opposition, however, must be understood in its context.

American Quakers experienced many changes and much dissension during the early 1820s, the time when Sarah was seeking recognition as a minister. The early simplicity of their chosen way of life had been affected by the rapidly changing culture of the nineteenth century. For example, many leaders of the Society of Friends experienced commercial and political success that clashed with the Quaker emphasis on plain living. They were faced with the decision of whether to adhere to their unique style of worship, dress, and speech or to abandon their peculiarities and integrate with mainstream American Protestantism. The rift between the Society of Friends factions eventually led to a decisive and bitter split in 1828.[81]

The two groups that emerged as a result of the Quaker schism came to be identified as the Orthodox and the Hicksites. The Orthodox were mostly urban dwellers who adopted a new system of belief that allowed them more doctrinal flexibility. They retained the

---

[80]Sarah Grimké, diary, quoted in Birney, 96. The male leaders of the Fourth and Arch Street Meeting, especially Elder Jonathan Evans, continually opposed Sarah and discouraged all her attempts to become a minister.

[81]Ingle, *Quakers in Conflict*, xii–xiv.

central elements of the Quaker faith while at the same time adjusting their teaching to the emerging urban, industrial age. In essence, this group adopted a belief system that would "allow them to participate in the affairs of the world without the tensions produced by an emphasis on quietism and fulfillment of a behavioral code."[82]

The opponents of the Orthodox group, the Hicksites, mostly resided in small towns and rural communities. Led by Elias Hicks, a Long Island farmer and Quaker minister, the Hicksites called for the preservation and restoration of traditional principles. They opposed a formal hierarchy and unrestrained secular activity and supported the maintenance of a strong and continuous tension between the believer and the world.[83]

In the late 1820s and early 1830s, the majority of Quakers in the Philadelphia area sided with the Hicksites.[84] Some of the prominent Quakers in Philadelphia, however, aligned themselves with the Orthodox. Conflict was inevitable. The conflict, however, was not due to theological differences but to a dispute over who would exercise power and moral authority in the Society of Friends. The dilemma over authority raised questions about the

---

[82]Robert W. Doherty, *The Hicksite Separation: A Sociological Analysis of Religious Schism in Early Nineteenth Century America* (New Brunswick NJ: Rutgers University Press, 1967) 31.

[83]Ibid., 32.

[84]In the Philadelphia area, the Hicksite Quakers slightly outnumbered the Orthodox Quakers. According to Robert Doherty, there were 378 Hicksites and 288 Orthodox Quakers in and around the city of Philadelphia. Endy, however, contends that the Hicksites held a two or three to one majority in the Philadelphia yearly meetings. Despite this dispute over exact numbers of Hicksite Quakers, the fact remains that the Hicksites held a clear majority in and around Philadelphia during the period that Sarah sought to become a Quaker minister. See Doherty, *The Hicksite Separation*, 49; and Endy, "The Society of Friends," 605.

appropriateness of including women and non-"birthright" Quakers in the power structures.[85]

The Orthodox group was dominated by male leaders, and they did not advocate female leadership in Quaker meetings. The group, therefore, did not produce many outstanding female leaders, and thus, the women members, for the most part, confined themselves to domestic duties and to acceptable benevolence activities. The Hicksite group, however, remained loyal to the older Quaker tradition of spiritual and vocational equality. Many Hicksite women had established themselves as leaders and ministers within their Quaker meeting.[86] The volatile dispute between the Orthodox and the Hicksite Quakers over the proper role of women within the Society of Friends occurred during the time in which Sarah sought to establish herself as a Quaker minister, and this factional dispute was most likely the cause for the opposition to her ministry.[87]

From her earliest association with the Quakers, Sarah had known only the Orthodox side of the faith. Her friends and acquaintances in Philadelphia were members of an Orthodox congregation. The leaders of the Fourth and Arch Street Meeting, champions of the Orthodox view, were not only threatened by the presence of a woman minister; they were also threatened, as was the entire Orthodox group, by any non-"birthright" Quaker attempting to gain positions of authority.[88] Thus, the Orthodox leaders became more exclusive, more rigid, and more suspicious of all but "birthright" Quakers.[89] Sarah, however, never recognized the profound impact that the dispute between the Orthodox and the

---

[85]"Birthright" Quakers were those who had been longstanding members of the Society of Friends, usually from birth. Non-"birthright" Quakers were those new to the Society.

[86]Lucretia Mott, Susan B. Anthony, Florence Kelley, and Alice Paul were all Hicksite Quakers. See Bacon, *Mothers of Feminism*, 92–94 and Hamm, *The Transformation of American Quakerism*, 47.

[87]Lerner, *The Grimké Sisters from South Carolina*, 61–62.

[88]Ibid.

[89]Ibid., 62.

Hicksite groups had on her own situation. Naive in the ways of organizational struggle and isolated from intellectual and social stimulation, she blamed herself when she failed to gain acceptance as a minister.[90]

Sarah's struggle to gain acceptance as a minister was complicated further when her closest Quaker friend and confidant, Israel Morris, proposed marriage. Morris's wife died in 1820, leaving him with eight children. The six boys and two girls ranged in age from five to twenty years. Sarah arrived in Philadelphia a year after Morris became a widower. Their mutual religious interests and their own personal sufferings drew them together. During this time, Sarah comforted and supported Morris just as he had done when she mourned her father's death.

The relationship slowly developed from a friendship based on mutual interests and support to one that was serious enough to warrant a marriage proposal. The details of their increasing affection for one another are not known because both Sarah and Morris eventually burned their letters to one another. Sarah's diaries, however, indicate that she had strong feelings for Morris and that his proposal tempted her.[91]

Morris first proposed to a thirty-three year old Sarah on September 16, 1826. Despite her deep affection for him, she declined his offer. She recorded her struggle with the decision in her diary: "How my poor soul pants for deliverance from the feelings of earthly attachment. Oh Lord, let not this grave swallow up and devour my soul, my life. I have no heart hardly for anything else [and] am not resigned to give Israel up yet. [I] see heavy trials to myself attendent [*sic*] upon our union from which I shrink."[92] Four years later, Morris repeated his marriage proposal and was once again rejected.[93] Given the evidence of Sarah's affection for Morris, what can account for her rejection of his proposal?

---

[90]Lerner, *The Feminist Thought of Sarah Grimké*, 10.

[91]Sarah Grimké, diary, 16 September 1830, 65; 11 September 1832, 46.

[92]Ibid., 11 September 1832, 46.

[93]Lerner, *The Feminist Thought of Sarah Grimké*, 11.

Sarah's diary does not contain a clear statement of the reasons behind her decision, but several factors may have played a role in her decision. First, Morris's children may have been opposed to his remarriage. Sarah referred to the children's opposition several times, but it seems unlikely that she and Morris would have been dissuaded from marriage simply because of his children's objections. Given the frequency of second marriages following the death of a spouse and the general acceptance of patriarchical dominance, such opposition from the children most likely could have been overcome. Thus, the children's objections would not have had much influence. Sarah also had established friendly relations with the children even before the death of their mother. She eventually could have gained their acceptance.[94]

Second, the existence of the children themselves may have contributed to Sarah's decision. Suddenly becoming a mother to eight children would have been overwhelming. Assuming such responsibility frightened Sarah. She wrote, "My soul shrunk from the fearful responsibility of such a situation."[95]

Third, Sarah repeatedly asserted that she could not accept "earthly love" because of her commitment to the ministry.[96] Apparently, she saw marriage to Morris as an obstacle to her goal of becoming a minister. Yet many Quaker women, including Sarah's friend Lucretia Mott, served as ministers and maintained a happy family life. The teachings of Quakerism certainly did not prohibit ministers from marrying.[97]

Fourth, Sarah's refusal may have been one more example of her lifelong practice of self-denial and self-renunciation. Repression of her own desires and needs came more easily to Sarah than their acceptance. The repeated denial of her education and career goals

---

[94]Lerner, *The Grimké Sisters from South Carolina*, 64.
[95]Sarah Grimké, diary, 16 September 1830, 65.
[96]Ibid.
[97]Lerner, *The Grimké Sisters from South Carolina*, 64.

may have had an impact on Sarah's ability to accept her desires as legitimate and obtainable.[98]

Fifth, Sarah's reluctance to marry may have been based on her fear of having to forfeit her hard-won independence from the traditional restrictions placed on women.[99] Conventional marriage in 1826 meant lifelong subordination for a woman. Having achieved already a sense of autonomy, Sarah perhaps hesitated in surrendering her newly found freedom.[100] The painful choice between sharing her life with a man she loved and maintaining her independence forced Sarah to recognize the importance of her self-identity and self-fulfillment.

All of the factors cited above may have played a part in Sarah's decision not to marry Morris. She certainly understood the demands that marriage and instant motherhood would place on her. After five years of living independently, such a drastic change in lifestyle frightened her. She had no guarantee that she could maintain a marriage relationship, mother eight children, and retain her newly found identity and purpose in life. Rather than take such a risk, Sarah remained unmarried. She made her decision despite the traditional expectations and pressures of her day. In the early nineteenth century, for a woman to remain single was cause for concern, and for a woman to turn down a marriage proposal, especially when she was in her thirties, was considered almost treasonous. By rejecting Morris's marriage proposal, Sarah once again rebelled against the social structures of her day.

In addition to the emotional distress Sarah experienced because of the marriage proposal and her rejection of it, she also was dealing with homesickness and guilt.[101] The decision to leave behind her family had been a difficult one, and the question of whether to remain in Philadelphia continued to trouble her.[102] The advice she

---

[98]Ibid., 64–65.

[99]Lerner, *The Feminist Thought of Sarah Grimké*, 11.

[100]Nies, *Seven Women*, 16.

[101]Sarah Grimké, diary, 6 October 1827, 31.

[102]Birney, *Sarah and Angelina Grimké*, 35.

received from her closest Quaker friends compounded her guilt. During Sarah's early years in Philadelphia, Catherine Morris especially insisted that Sarah should return to Charleston to fulfill her duty of caring for her aging mother. Her living arrangements and her commitment to her Quaker beliefs made Sarah vulnerable to these pressures. Even though she was not eager to return to the isolated and repressive life of Charleston, she felt compelled to return home, and so in mid-1827, at the age of thirty-four, Sarah made plans to travel to Charleston.[103]

Although the return home may not have been Sarah's idea or even her desire, her concern for her mother's spiritual welfare made the decision to return a bearable one. Sarah's perception of Mary Grimké's lack of spirituality had long grieved her, and a trip to Charleston would enable Sarah to guide her mother in the ways of true religion.[104] The trip also would provide an opportunity for Sarah to restore harmony with her family. Time away from Philadelphia also would allow a reprieve from the growing discomfort she experienced during Quaker meetings, which increasingly left her "in a cold and indifferent state."[105] She believed that by removing herself from the Fourth and Arch Street Meeting she would have the opportunity to clarify her feelings toward the Society of Friends.

Sarah's departure, however, did not signal an abandonment of her commitment to Quakerism. She returned to Charleston committed to the beliefs and practices of the Quaker faith. Her adoption of the full Quaker dress just prior to her departure to Charleston indicated the extent of Sarah's commitment to Quakerism. She began to wear plainer clothes during her earliest days as a Quaker, but she had not adopted the traditional Quaker style of dress. Convinced that God was unconcerned about her manner of dress but also convinced that her clothing had become an

---

[103]Du Pre Lumpkin, *The Emancipation of Angelina Grimké*, 26–27.

[104]Birney, *Sarah and Angelina Grimké*, 36.

[105]Sarah Grimké, diary, quoted in Lerner, *The Grimké Sisters from South Carolina*, 61.

obstacle for her spiritual development, Sarah discontinued wearing elaborate black dresses and arrayed herself in the drab and somber Quaker dresses. Her change in fashion also may have occurred because of her concern that her family take seriously her commitment to Quakerism.[106]

Sarah arrived in Charleston late in the autumn of 1827. For several weeks she enjoyed the warmth and affection of her family and the familiar routine of charitable involvement and Quaker meetings. Even though the Grimké family warmly welcomed Sarah home, they did not sympathize with her new lifestyle nor did they respond positively to her attempts to convert them.[107] Indeed, Sarah's new religious commitment deeply offended the Grimkés. They objected to her "sober Quaker dress, her suppressed demeanor, her frowns at display, her outspoken stern reminders, her withdrawals to her chamber to engage in private religious devotions, and finally her refusal to join her family in common worship either at home or in their churches."[108] Sarah's presence increased the tension between her and her family and had little effect on her mother's spiritual condition. Indeed, Mary Grimké rebuffed all of Sarah's efforts to steer her toward Quakerism. Mary continued to cling to "spiritual darkness," and the Grimké household continued to be quarrelsome and contentious.[109]

Meanwhile, Sarah's steadfast commitment to Quakerism appeared threatened. In the comfort and security of her childhood home, she found it difficult to maintain her Quaker beliefs and habits.[110] After eight months of conflict with her family and struggling with her own conscience, Sarah abandoned her hope that her family would accept the teachings of Quakerism, and she decided to return to the North. On 20 April 1828, she set sail for

---

[106]Sarah Grimké, diary, 14 November 1828, n.p.

[107]Ibid., 22 November 1827, 42.

[108]Du Pre Lumpkin, *The Emancipation of Angelina Grimké*, 28.

[109]Sarah Grimké, diary, 9 December 1828, 45; 22 December 1828, 46.

[110]Ibid., 12 December 1828, 44; 22 December 1828, 46; 13 January 1828, 50.

Philadelphia.[111] Even though Sarah's visit to Charleston did not produce the desired results, her visit was not completely unsuccessful. Her presence in Charleston played an instrumental part in the eventual conversion of her youngest sister, Angelina, to Quakerism.[112]

The closeness that existed between Sarah and her younger sister from the time of Angelina's birth had not been diminished by their years apart. Sarah's return to Charleston delighted Angelina, and the two spent many hours together during Sarah's eight-month visit. The twenty-two-year-old Angelina proved to be a worthy debate partner for Sarah, and most of their debates concerned Quaker beliefs. Sarah shared her convictions about her call to the ministry and to a plain lifestyle, and she encouraged Angelina to repent and to forsake erroneous religious doctrines.[113]

Angelina's own spiritual pilgrimage mirrored Sarah's early struggles. Dissatisfied with the teachings and practices of the Episcopal Church, Angelina refused confirmation at the age of thirteen.[114] During the next seven years, she experienced profound spiritual frustration. Organized religion seemed oppressive and meaningless to her, and she turned to charitable activities to fill the void. In April 1826, Angelina, like Sarah had before her, became a Presbyterian. Within the Presbyterian Church, she found acceptance as well as opportunities to participate actively.[115] Yet Angelina's spiritual pilgrimage differed somewhat from that of her older sister. Angelina never suffered total despondency and emotional fluctuations, and her commitment to the church brought her peace and satisfaction. Angelina's new faith inspired and satisfied her, and her conversion brought with it the conviction that she had been

[111]Ibid., 15 February 1828, 57.
[112]Ibid., 11 January 1828, 49–50.
[113]Ibid., 6 January 1828, 49; 11 January 1828, 49–50.
[114]Theodore Weld, *In Memory: Angelina Grimké Weld* (Boston: George Ellis, 1880) 35.
[115]Birney, *Sarah and Angelina Grimké*, 20–23.

called to fulfill some great mission.[116] As the months passed, however, she recognized that the Presbyterian Church obstructed her search for that mission. Angelina not only began to doubt the Presbyterian Church's acceptance and support of her; she began to question the Church's stance on slavery.

From childhood, Angelina, like Sarah, had been appalled by the conditions of slaves. As she matured, she continued to oppose slavery and to work for improved treatment for the Grimké slaves. As a young woman, Angelina questioned the Southern churches' refusal to attack the system that promoted slavery. Especially disappointing was her own Presbyterian minister's refusal to speak out against slavery.[117] By the time of Sarah's visit to Charleston in the autumn of 1827, Angelina was confused and disillusioned. The Presbyterian Church, just like the Episcopal Church, had not lived up to her early expectations. Thus, Sarah found in Angelina a receptive and somewhat vulnerable listener and set out to lead her younger sister to convert to Quakerism. Much to Sarah's disappointment, Angelina did not convert during Sarah's visit home.[118]

After Sarah left Charleston in the spring of 1828 to return to Philadelphia, Angelina began to consider seriously the tenets of Quakerism. Within a few weeks, she withdrew from the Presbyterian Church and began attending Quaker meetings. Despite the fact that the Charleston Quaker congregation now consisted only of two quarrelsome elderly men, Angelina continued to attend the meetings and to look to Quakerism as a source of comfort and peace. A visit to Philadelphia in July 1828 finally convinced Angelina that Quakerism was the "true religion." Time in the North also strengthened her antislavery views and her appreciation of the Northern lifestyle. She marveled at the success of a society founded on the free labor system and relished the freedom of movement she

---

[116]Angelina Grimké, diary, January 10, 1828, in Ceplair, *The Public Years*, 16.

[117]Weld, *In Memory*, 37.

[118]Sarah Grimké, diary, 29 November 1827, 43.

experienced during her days in Philadelphia.[119] The visit confirmed for Angelina that she too could no longer remain in the oppressive atmosphere of the South.

Angelina returned to Charleston in the late summer of 1828 and remained there until November 1829. She was reluctant to leave her family because she considered her presence their only hope for salvation from false Christianity. Like Sarah, Angelina determined to convert her family to Quakerism. Yet the commitment to remain in Charleston proved to be useless because her family showed no signs of accepting Quakerism. Angelina's increasing frustration over her family's rebuffs, her growing impatience with the Southern attitude toward slavery, and the increasing pressure placed on her by Sarah to relocate in Philadelphia finally led Angelina to leave her family and move to the North.[120]

Sarah's pressure on Angelina cannot be attributed simply to concern for Angelina's spiritual condition. In the spring and summer of 1829, Sarah experienced great loneliness and continued rejection. Her attempts at Quaker ministry were rebuffed repeatedly at the Fourth and Arch Street Meeting. Although she continued to strive toward her goal of being a Quaker minister, the congregation to which she belonged refused to recognize her efforts.[121] Now bitter as well as lonely, only the prospect of Angelina's joining her gave Sarah any hope that she would ever be freed from her "solitary path" and from the "fiery trial" she was enduring.[122] Sarah's obvious pain and frantic pleas convinced Angelina that she must join her older sister. In October 1829, the twenty-four year old Angelina finally arrived in Philadelphia.

Angelina's presence had a calming effect on her older sister. Together they lived quietly and somewhat contently for several years in the home of Catherine Morris. Angelina applied for and

---

[119]Lerner, *The Grimké Sisters from South Carolina*, 74, 87–88.

[120]Angelina Grimké, diary, September 11, 1829, in Ceplair, The Public Years, 18.

[121]Birney, *Sarah and Angelina Grimké*, 94.

[122]Sarah Grimké, diary, 12 July 1829, 29.

was granted membership in the Fourth and Arch Street Meeting on 4 March 1831, eighteen months after her arrival in Philadelphia.[123] Eventually, Angelina concluded that she, like Sarah, had been called to be a Quaker minister. Yet, unlike Sarah, Angelina did not quietly accept the Society of Friends' restrictions on her activities or her goals. She regularly criticized the shortcomings of the Society of Friends and promptly responded to all criticism against her and against Sarah. The Quakers reacted to Angelina's outspokenness by pressuring her to return to Charleston and to fulfill her daughterly duty to her mother.[124] Sarah intervened in the dispute between the Quaker leadership and her younger sister and volunteered to return to Charleston to care for their mother. The compromise satisfied the leaders, and in late 1830, Sarah, at the age of thirty-eight, returned to Charleston, a visit that proved to be her last. She remained at home for a year.[125]

During Sarah's absence from Philadelphia, Angelina moved from Catherine Morris's home to live with her sister Anna. The freedom resulting from the move allowed Angelina to become more involved in a relationship with Edward Bettle, a young Quaker man. It also allowed her to explore the possibility of attending Catherine Beecher's training school for teachers in Hartford, Connecticut.[126] Angelina's conduct resulted in even further reproof by the Quaker leadership. Although leaders of the Society of Friends condoned her relationship with Bettle, they frowned upon what appeared to be inappropriate behavior. They insisted on proper supervision during courtship, and they believed that Angelina had disregarded Quaker

[123]Lerner, *The Grimké Sisters from South Carolina*, 89.

[124]Angelina Grimké, diary, July 20, 1830, in Ceplair, *The Public Years*, 18–19.

[125]Du Pre Lumpkin, *The Emancipation of Angelina Grimké*, 63–64.

[126]Ibid. Catherine Beecher was the eldest daughter of Lyman Beecher and the sister of Harriet Beecher Stowe. In 1827, Catherine established a Female Seminary at Hartford, Connecticut. The seminary's early emphasis was on women's primary profession—housework and homemaking. Later, she incorporated teacher training into the seminary's curriculum.

guidelines. They also disapproved of her desire to attend a non-Quaker school that would force her to associate with members of other denominations.[127]

By the time Sarah returned to Philadelphia in September 1831, Angelina's membership within the Society of Friends was in jeopardy. Sarah's presence and Angelina's return to live in Morris's home, however, lessened the severe strain between the Quaker leaders and Angelina. The death of Bettle in late 1832 spared Angelina from alienating herself further from the Society. She earlier had realized that she could not marry Bettle, and her rejection of the son of a prominent Orthodox Quaker family would not have endeared her to members of the Society.[128] Sarah advised and counseled Angelina during this period. She encouraged her younger sister to accept and to follow the Quaker teachings and practices. Yet the Society of Friends' treatment of her younger sister disappointed Sarah. Both sisters were beginning to feel less comfortable with the restrictive demands placed on them by the Society.

The Grimké sisters' dissatisfaction with the Society of Friends resulted not only because of their discomfort with the restrictive nature of the Quakers but was also a reflection of their increasing anti-institutional outlook. At this time in their lives, both Sarah and Angelina began to voice their suspicion that most human institutions maintained their authority by force or violence. They pointed to the existence of slavery and of male domination of women to justify their suspicion. The Grimkés' move toward an anti-institutional

---

[127]The reasons cited by the Society of Friends for instructing Angelina to abandon her plans to attend the Beecher school included the fact that she would be living among strangers, leaving her sisters, and abandoning her charitable work. Perhaps the true reason, and the one that remained unstated, was that the Quakers feared that this impressionable young woman would revert back to Presbyterianism if she associated with persons of that denominational persuasion. See Birney, *Sarah and Angelina Grimké*, 109.

[128]Du Pre Lumpkin, *The Emancipation of Angelina Grimké*, 69.

position perhaps led them to be more receptive to involvement in the abolition movement.

The American abolition movement made a significant step forward on 4 December 1833. On that date in the city of Philadelphia, the American Anti-Slavery Society officially was founded. This national society adopted as its primary goal the immediate emancipation of slaves.[129] The founding of this society resulted in antislavery sentiment sweeping quickly through the Northern cities, including Philadelphia. Within a few days, twenty women in that city founded the Philadelphia Female Anti-Slavery Society.[130] The excitement and controversy that these societies caused did not go unnoticed by two of Philadelphia's citizens: Sarah and Angelina Grimké.

The founding in 1833 of the two antislavery societies, however, was not the Grimké sisters' introduction to abolition. Sarah began reading antislavery literature years before the formation of the societies and passed the literature on to Angelina.[131] By early 1834, Angelina had become a regular reader of the abolitionist papers such as William Lloyd Garrison's *The Liberator* and the Anti-Slavery Society's *Emancipator*.[132] Her literary introduction to abolition and her growing commitment to the idea of immediate emancipation eventually led her to attend her first antislavery lecture. On the evening of 3 March 1835, Angelina attended the lecture of George Thompson, a British abolitionist. Her presence at the meeting directly defied the Fourth and Arch Street leaders' position and Sarah's advice. Within a month after her presence at the lecture,

---

[129]Dwight Dumond, *Antislavery: The Crusade for Freedom in America* (Ann Arbor: University of Michigan Press, 1961) 199.

[130]Blanche Glassman Hersh, *The Slavery of Sex: Feminist-Abolitionists in America* (Urbana: University of Illinois Press, 1978) 14.

[131]Birney, *Sarah and Angelina Grimké*, 91.

[132]Du Pre Lumpkin, *The Emancipation of Angelina Grimké*, 72.

Angelina officially joined the Philadelphia Female Anti-Slavery Society.[133]

The decision to become involved in such a radical movement—a movement denounced by the Orthodox leaders of Angelina's meeting and questioned by her older sister—was a difficult one. Sarah's opposition to involvement in the antislavery movement proved especially troubling. Sarah had not abandoned her opposition to slavery nor was she unwilling to involve herself in eradicating slavery. Indeed, since 1829, Sarah had contributed financially to the American Colonization Society, participated in the Free Product Movement, and continually pleaded with her mother to free the Grimké slaves.[134] Yet Sarah was reluctant to involve herself or to support her sister's participation in an abolition society. Her reluctance may be attributed to her understanding that association with the Anti-Slavery Society would alienate her from the Society of Friends. In 1834, Sarah continued to be committed to Quakerism despite the treatment she received from her fellow Quakers. She hoped to remain within Quakerism and to lead in the reformation of its practices and prejudices. Thus, she responded negatively to Angelina's push toward involvement in abolition. Sarah's opposition to involvement in the antislavery movement, however, was short-lived.

During the period in which Angelina became increasingly interested in the abolition movement, Sarah faced continual rejection from the Orthodox Elders. After many years of struggling to establish herself as a minister, Sarah, who was now forty-three years old, finally conceded that her goal was unattainable. Giving up her goal, however, meant also giving up her commitment to Quakerism. The decisive event that led her to this decision occurred

---

[133]Keith E. Melder, *Beginnings of Sisterhood: The American Woman's Rights Movement, 1800–1850,* Studies in the Life of Women, ed. Gerda Lerner (New York: Schocken Books, 1977) 78.

[134]P. J. Staudenraus, *The African Colonization Movement, 1816–1855* (New York: Columbia University Press, 1961) 126. See also Lerner, The Grimké Sisters from South Carolina, 131.

in August 1836. She described the event in a letter to Theodore Weld, dated March 10, 1837:

> A circumstance occurred that has proved the means of releasing me from those bonds which almost destroyed my mind. As I was speaking one day in mtg. the Friend who rules in our Yearly Meeting rose in the meeting and desired me to desist in these words: "Perhaps the Fd. may be satisfied now." I of course instantly resumed my seat and never felt more peaceful, and the conviction then arose that my bonds were broken. The act on the part of this Elder was entirely unprecedented and unsanctioned by our Discipline but his power is undisputed. I cannot give thee any idea of the spiritual bondage I have been in; but notwithstanding this my heart clung to the Society of Friends and the struggle to give them up, to resign the cherished hope of being permitted to preach among them the unsearchable riches of Christ has been very great; but that has past and peaceful resignation cloathes [*sic*] my spirit.[135]

The Elder who suggested that Sarah stop speaking was Jonathan Edwards, the most powerful member of the Philadelphia Orthodoxy. Within the Society of Friends, no established or recognized rule allowed for disrupting the utterance of any member. Edwards's act, therefore, was most likely a personal rebuke of Sarah rather than an act of discipline. His disruption also was an abuse of power. Knowing that no member would have dared to confront his clear violation of the understood rules, Edwards used his authority as a leader to carry out his own desire to hamper Sarah's ministry.

The incident with Edwards proved to be the breaking point. Sarah no longer felt that she must remain loyal or subordinate to the Quaker leadership. Edwards's censure released Sarah from her ties

---

[135]Gilbert H. Barnes and Dwight L. Dumond, eds. *Letters of Theodore Dwight Weld, Angelina Grimké Weld, and Sarah Grimké, 1822–1844* (New York: Da Capo Press, 1970) 1:373.

to the Society of Friends and from her commitment to the ministry.[136] Her newly acquired freedom was accompanied by a sense of relief that the continual opposition to her attempts at becoming a minister were finally over.

Sarah also experienced relief in being freed from teachings and practices that she had found to be oppressive and restrictive, especially the views of Orthodox Quakers on racial segregation and abolition. Despite the early involvement of the Society of Friends in opposing slavery, blacks were not admitted to membership in meetings until 1796. In that year, the Philadelphia Yearly Meeting attempted to overcome its contradictory position on equality by agreeing to accept applications for membership without "distinction of color." The decision opened the way for some blacks within the Society of Friends to become full members. Yet even this decision did not bring full equality to black Quakers. Most meeting houses retained "Negro benches" or "Negro pews," which were separate benches set aside for blacks.[137] The Fourth and Arch Street Meeting practiced such racial segregation. In her 1839 "Letter on the Subject of Prejudice Amongst the Society of Friends in the United States," Sarah described her disappointment with such blatant prejudice. She denounced the unwillingness of the Quakers to associate with blacks, and she revealed the predominance of the use of a "Negro pew" in Quaker meetings:

> There is a bench set apart for the coloured people at our meetings, but there is no record of it on our minutes. This is the case both in the city and the country, as *far as I know*. In the city, there is a committee "to sit among the youth, and keep order in the meeting," provide seats for strangers, etc. A part of this committee have the charge of the coloured bench. Still I have seen white persons occasionally sitting on it, either from ignorance or for the sake of convenience, but

---

[136]Ibid.

[137]Ceplair, *The Public Years*, 15.

never near the prescribed class, except a crowded meeting rendered it unavoidable.[138]

Eventually, as Sarah and Angelina began to understand and to protest against the racial prejudice they found in Quaker meetings, they began to sit on the "Negro pew" as a sign of their protest of the existence of such a bench.

Sarah's decision in 1836 to separate herself from the Society of Friends was traumatic. Yet her decision proved to be a liberating experience. It freed Sarah from the continual criticism and rejection she had encountered; it freed her from the prejudicial practices of the Quakers; and it freed her to look for other avenues to fulfill her call to ministry.

---

[138]Sarah Grimké, "Letter on the Subject of Prejudice Amongst the Society of Friends in the United States," 1839, Sarah Grimké Papers, Boston Public Library, Boston, MA, p. 7.

Chapter 4

Abolitionism:
Sarah Grimké's Commitment to
Combat the Institution of Slavery

Throughout the colonial period and after the American Revolution, most Americans accepted slavery as a normal and inevitable part of life. As a working institution, however, slavery gradually became confined to Southern states. Americans in only that one region had an economic stake in its perpetuation. Eventually, some Americans began to express their objections to slavery, and they began to work together to abolish slavery. Many of Americans who joined in this early struggle against slavery were members of the religious communities rather than political parties, and the Society of Friends was among the earliest of those religious communities to renounce slavery and to establish antislavery societies. As early as 1688, the Quakers denounced slavery and the slave trade. By 1776, some annual Quaker meetings began taking bolder steps by calling on all members to treat blacks with impartiality and by directing local meetings to disown members who refused to free their slaves.[1]

---

[1]Thomas E. Drake, *Quakers and Slavery in America* (New Haven: Yale University Press, 1950) 72.

In addition to official proclamations by the Society of Friends, individual Quakers provided leadership in the fight against slavery. Beginning in 1811, Elias Hicks published pamphlets that denounced the use of slave-produced products and called on fellow Quakers to boycott such products. In 1816, Benjamin Lundy formed the first Ohio antislavery organization, the Union Humane Society, and in 1821, he began publishing the *Genius of Universal Emancipation*, a monthly Quaker newspaper completely devoted to the cause of abolition.[2] The newspaper gained widespread circulation quickly, making Lundy the first really effective force in the antislavery movement in the United States. Another of Lundy's contributions was his work in establishing and publicizing "free produce stores" that sold only goods grown or manufactured by means of non-slave labor.[3] The establishment of these stores was an attempt to weaken the economic profitability of slavery.

The Quakers also were instrumental in organizing the first American abolition societies. They were leaders in the formation of the Pennsylvania Society for Promoting the Abolition of Slavery, the Relief of Negroes Unlawfully Held in Bondage, Improving the Conditions of the African Race (1775); the American Convention for Promoting the Abolition of Slavery and Improving the Conditions of the African Race (1794); the American Colonization Society (1816); and the Pennsylvania Free Produce Association (1827).[4]

The sentiments of the Quakers soon spread beyond their own circles and influenced persons such as Henry Clay, James Madison, and John Marshall. These prestigious leaders held membership in the American Colonization Society (ACS). The ACS was formed in 1817 in order to transport free blacks back to Africa, and in 1822,

---

[2]Merton L. Dillon, *Benjamin Lundy and the Struggle for Negro Freedom* (Urbana/ London: University of Illinois Press, 1966) 45–46.

[3]Robert William Fogel, *Without Consent or Contract: The Rise and Fall of American Slavery* (New York: W. W. Norton and Company, 1989) 251.

[4]Drake, *Quakers and Slavery*, 90, 108, 124–26, 171.

the ACS established a colony on the west coast of Africa. In 1847, this colony became the independent nation of Liberia. Ultimately, however, this method of ridding the country of slavery proved unsuccessful. By 1830, only 1,421 persons had relocated in Liberia, [5] slavery had been extended further west, and many people had begun to articulate frustration with the gradual approach to ending slavery. Eventually, some of the most notable members of the ACS—including Arthur and Lewis Tappan, Theodore Dwight Weld, Gerrit Smith, Amos Phelps, and James Birney—withdrew from the organization and dedicated themselves to the cause of "immediate emancipation."[6]

The "immediate emancipation" movement called for the earlier, ineffective abolitionism to be repudiated and for men and women to be united in a vigorous, new attempt to abolish slavery.[7]

---

[5]P. J. Staudenraus, *The African Colonization Movement, 1816–1855* (New York: Columbia University Press, 1961) 251. See also Dwight Lowell Dumond, *Antislavery Origins of the Civil War in the United States* (Ann Arbor: University of Michigan Press, 1939) 11; and Merton L. Dillon, "The Failure of the American Abolitionists," *Journal of Southern History* 25/2 (May 1959): 165–66.

[6]For further reading on these abolitionist leaders, see Bertram Wyatt-Brown, *Lewis Tappan and the Evangelical War against Slavery* (Cleveland: The Press of Case Western Reserve University, 1969); Rebecca J. Winter, *The Night Cometh: Two Wealthy Evangelicals Face the Nation* (South Pasadena CA: William Carey Library, 1977); Benjamin P. Thomas, *Theodore Weld: Crusader for Freedom* (New Brunswick NJ: Rutgers University Press, 1950); Robert H. Abzug, *Passionate Liberator: Theodore Dwight Weld and the Dilemma of Reform* (New York: Oxford University Press, 1980); Ralph Volney Harlow, *Gerrit Smith: Philanthropist and Reformer* (New York: Henry Holt and Company, 1939); Octavius Brooks Frothingham, *Gerrit Smith: A Biography* (New York: Negro Universities Press, 1969); and William Birney, *James G. Birney and His Times: The Genesis of the Republican Party with Some Account of Abolition Movements in the South before 1828* (New York: Negro Universities Press, 1969).

[7]For Amos Phelps' extended definition of immediate emancipation, see "Amos A. Phelps Supports Immediate Action," *The Antislavery Argument,*

The move away from gradual emancipation and the decline of gradualist societies, according to James Birney, "may be ascribed to this defect,—they did not inflexibly ask for *immediate* emancipation."[8] Thus, by the early 1830s, abolition, with its emphasis on immediatism and its insistence that all ties with the previous attempts at abolition be broken, differed from the antislavery movement that preceded it. Several factors or influences may be cited for this shift in attitude from a gradualist approach to emancipation to an immediatist approach: the British abolitionists, revivalism, and William Lloyd Garrison.

First, the British Society for the Mitigation and Gradual Abolition of Slavery, an organization that in 1830 adopted immediatism, influenced the abandonment of gradualism in America. Its distinguished members included William Wilberforce, Thomas Clarkson, Elizabeth Heyrick, Charles Stuart, and George Thompson. These British abolitionists wrote and distributed pamphlets especially aimed at American audiences, sent speakers to tour American cities, and called on the British Foreign Office to pressure the American government into legislating immediate emancipation.[9]

Second, in 1824, a revival began in upstate New York under the leadership of Charles G. Finney. In his preaching, Finney emphasized personal moral reform as the best means by which to achieve social reform. Reformed sinners, he said, should strive to be "useful in the highest degrees possible."[10] They must be committed

---

ed. William H. Pease and Jane H. Pease (Indianapolis: Bobbs-Merrill Co., 1965) 71–85.

[8][James G. Birney], *Correspondence between the Hon. F. H. Elmore, One of the South Carolina Delegation in Congress, and James G. Birney* (New York, 1838) 8; quoted in Ronald G. Walters, *The Antislavery Appeal: American Abolitionism After 1830* (Baltimore: Johns Hopkins University Press, 1976) 1, n. 1.

[9]Fogel, *Without Consent or Contract*, 234–35.

[10]Charles Grandison Finney, *Lectures on Revival of Religion*, ed. William J. McLoughlin (Cambridge MA: Belknap, 1960) 404.

to making the world a fit place for the imminent return of Christ. They also must be committed to "the universal reformation of the world" and to the "complete and final overthrow" of "war, slavery, licentiousness, and all such evils and abominations."[11] With regard to slavery, Finney preached vivid sermons condemning the practice, and he refused to serve communion to slave-owners.[12] He denounced slavery as a national sin and asserted that only full emancipation of slaves would rectify this horrific evil.[13] Despite his strong views about slavery, Finney never joined an abolition society. His preaching and his influence, however, resulted in many of his followers, particularly Theodore Dwight Weld, joining the cause of immediatism.[14]

---

[11]Charles Finney, quoted in William G. McLoughlin, *Revivals, Awakenings, and Reform: An Essay on Religion and Social Change in America, 1607–1977*, Chicago History of American Religion, ed. Martin E. Marty (Chicago: University of Chicago Press, 1978) 129. See also Anne C. Loveland, "Evangelicalism and 'Immediate Emancipation' in American Antislavery Thought," *Journal of Southern History* 32/2 (May 1966): 178–79.

[12]The reason Finney gave for not associating himself with the abolition movement was that his primary concern was evangelism. Abolitionists such as Lewis Tappan accused Finney of cowardice for not actively pursuing his conviction that slavery must be ended. Weld, however, defended Finney, by writing: "God has called some prophets, some apostles, some teachers. All the members of the body of Christ have not the same office." Theodore Dwight Weld to Lewis Tappan, 17 November 1835, in Gilbert H. Barnes and Dwight L. Dumond, eds., *Letters of Theodore Dwight Weld, Angelina Grimké Weld, and Sarah Grimké, 1822–1844* (New York: Da Capo Press, 1970) 1:243. See also Abzug, *Passionate Liberator*, 155.

[13]Charles E. Hambrick-Stowe, *Charles G. Finney and the Spirit of American Evangelicalism* (Grand Rapids: Wm. B. Eerdmans Publishing Company, 1996) 141.

[14]Alice Felt Tyler, *Freedom's Ferment: Phases of American Social History from the Colonial Period to the Outbreak of the Civil War* (New York: Harper and Brothers, 1944) 41.

A final, and perhaps the most significant, factor in the spread of immediatism was the leadership of William Lloyd Garrison.[15] Garrison was not the first to embrace "immediate emancipation," but his passionate and militant support of the cause thrust immediatism to the forefront of the abolitionist movement.[16] In 1831, Garrison organized the New England Anti-Slavery Society and began publishing *The Liberator,* and with these events, immediate emancipation rapidly became the primary thrust of the abolition movement.[17]

From the beginning of his work as an abolitionist, Garrison made a special effort to gain the support and the sympathy of women for the abolition cause, and in 1831, when he began distributing *The Liberator,* he purposefully included a column especially for women readers. The "ladies section" had a picture of a slave woman kneeling in chains, and under the picture was the caption, "Am I Not A Woman And A Sister?" In his weekly column, Garrison implored his female readers "to weep, and speak, and act" on behalf of the "degraded and insufferable condition" of

----

[15]See John Jay Chapman, *William Lloyd Garrison*, 2d ed. (Boston: Atlantic Monthly, 1921); John Thomas, *The Liberator: William Lloyd Garrison, A Biography* (Boston: Little, Brown, 1963); and Walter M. Merrill, *Against Wind and Tide: A Biography of Wm. Lloyd Garrison* (Cambridge: Harvard University Press, 1963).

[16]William E. Cain, ed., *William Lloyd Garrison and the Fight Against Slavery: Selections from The Liberator* (Boston/New York: Bedford Books of St. Martin's Press, 1995) 10–12.

[17]Louis Filler, *The Crusade Against Slavery, 1830–1860* (New York: Harper and Row, 1960) 60. For further explanations of the move from gradualism to immediatism, see David Brion Davis, "The Emergence of Immediatism in British and American Antislavery Thought," *Mississippi Valley Historical Review* 49/2 (September 1962): 209–30. Davis cites natural rights philosophy, the weakness of American political institutions, the recognition of slavery as sin, and the failure of gradualism as all contributing to the call for immediate emancipation of slaves. See also Loveland, "Evangelicalism and 'Immediate Emancipation'," 172–88.

members of their own sex.[18] Other voices besides that of Garrison called for female equality within the abolition movement, and some of those voices were heard a full decade before the "woman question" controversy became a disruptive issue within the immediatist campaign.[19] These voices belonged to remarkable and gifted women.

One women who raised the "woman question" and who wrote numerous articles encouraging women to take an active role in the antislavery crusade was Elizabeth Margaret Chandler. Chandler, a Philadelphia Quaker and a co-worker of Benjamin Lundy, began contributing abolitionist articles to *The Genius of Universal Emancipation* in 1826. Three years later, she became the editor of its "Ladies Repository" section. In some of her earliest articles, she implored women to organize antislavery societies, to speak out against slavery, and to use whatever abilities they possessed to combat "evil." Though not consciously a feminist, Chandler stressed that women, as the more sensitive and sympathetic sex, were the natural foes of slavery and thus had a special obligation because members of their own sex were in bondage. Her emphasis on the plight of slave women reflected her belief that women were especially victimized by slavery because of their vulnerability to sexual abuse.[20]

Other women soon followed the lead of Chandler and dedicated themselves to the cause of abolition. In 1832, Maria

[18]*The Liberator*, 7 January 1832.

[19]Keith E. Melder, *Beginning of Sisterhood: The American Woman's Rights Movement, 1800–1850,* Studies in the Life of Women, ed. Gerda Lerner (New York: Shocken Books, 1977) 108–10. See also Dorothy C. Bass, "'The Best Hopes of the Sexes': The Woman Question in Garrisonian Abolitionism" (Ph.D. diss., Brown University, 1980) 1–3.

[20]Blanche Glassman Hersh, "'Am I Not a Woman and a Sister?' Abolitionist Beginning of Nineteenth-Century Feminism," in *Antislavery Reconsidered: New Perspectives on the Abolitionists, eds. Lewis Perry and Michael Fellmen* (Baton Rouge: Louisiana State University Press, 1979) 256.

Weston Chapman and three of her sisters (Caroline, Anne, and Deborah) organized the Boston Female Anti-Slavery Society. As the moving force behind this organization, Maria Chapman worked tirelessly on fundraising, scheduling antislavery fairs, and editing *Liberty Bell,* a book of articles and poems by well-known abolitionists.[21]

Chapman, however, was not content limiting her work to serving as a leader of a female reform organization. Her friends and her enemies knew her to be an imposing and domineering woman, one who continually battled against the limitations placed on her and on women in general.[22] Thus, it did not surprise many of her contemporaries when she assumed the "male" role of propagandist and agitator. She initiated petition campaigns and edited *The Liberator* during Garrison's frequent absences.[23] In broadening her sphere of influence, Chapman lived out what had become a constant theme in her writings and speeches—that women, as moral beings, had an obligation to oppose slavery and to speak freely against it whenever the opportunity arose.[24]

Another woman who championed the cause of abolition while also asserting the rights of women to lead this movement was Lydia Maria Child. Child was a respected author of guidebooks and popular history and the editor of a favorite children's magazine *The Juvenile Miscellany.* Her activism as an abolitionist and her advocacy of human rights, including women's rights, led to the destruction of her already established writing career.[25]

In 1833, Child published her first antislavery work, *An Appeal in Favor of Americans Called Africans*. This was the first important

---

[21]Ibid., 259.

[22]Blanch Glassman Hersh, *The Slavery of Sex: Feminist-Abolitionists in America* (Urbana: University of Illinois Press, 1978) 11.

[23]Hersh, "Am I Not a Woman and a Sister?" 258–59.

[24]Maria Weston Chapman, *Right or Wrong in Massachusetts* (Boston: Dow and Jackson's Anti-Slavery Press, 1839; reprint, New York: Negro Universities Press, 1969) 12–13.

[25]Hersh, *The Slavery of Sex*, 13.

abolitionist writing by a woman, and it was the first book written by an American advocating immediate abolition.[26] The publication of the book brought both public criticism and insults that eventually led to the loss of much of her previous audience.[27] Such abusive treatment did not surprise Child. She had anticipated it. In the preface to her *Appeal*, she wrote:

> I am fully aware of the unpopularity of the task I have undertaken; but though I expect ridicule and censure, I do not fear them.
> A few years hence, the opinion of the world will be a matter in which I have not even the most transient interest; but this book will be abroad on its mission of humanity long after the hand that wrote it is mingling with the dust.
> Should it be the means of advancing, even one single hour, the inevitable progress of truth and justice, I would not exchange the consciousness for all Rothchild's wealth, or Sir Walter's fame.[28]

Two years later Child turned her attention to the status and treatment of women. In 1835, she published a two-volume work titled *History of the Condition of Women, in Various Ages and Nations* in which she explored the status of women around the world. She examined marriage customs, property laws, educational and vocational opportunities, and discrimination experienced by

---

[26]Glenna Matthews "'Little Women' Who Helped Make this Great War," in *Why the Civil War Came*, ed. Gabor S. Boritt (New York/Oxford: Oxford University Press, 1996) 37.

[27]Samuel Sillen, *Women Against Slavery* (New York: Masses and Mainstream, 1955) 41.

[28]L. Maria Child, *An Appeal in Behalf of Americans Called Africans* (New York: John S. Taylor, 1836; reprint, New York: Arno Press and New York Times, 1968) 3.

women.[29] Following the publication of her *History*, Child went on to produce over thirty abolition books and pamphlets. She eventually became the editor of the *National Anti-Slavery Standard*, the weekly newspaper of the Anti-Slavery Society.

Chandler, Chapman, Child, and countless other women made considerable contributions to the abolition cause. By providing leadership in the effort to end slavery, they also called attention to the rights and the abilities of women. Despite their hard work, substantial writings, and remarkable leadership, no women were invited to participate in the organizational meeting of the American Anti-Slavery Society held in December 1833 in Philadelphia. On the second day of the convention, the sixty male delegates from eleven states reconsidered the exclusion of women and promptly extended an invitation to four women: Lucretia Mott, Esther Moore, Lydia White, and Sydney Ann Lee. The invitation to the historic assembly, however, was conditional. The women were to be "listeners and spectators," not participants.[30]

One of the women invited to the convention, however, did not confine herself to being merely a "listener and spectator." Lucretia Mott spoke out several times, proposing effective solutions to the organizational problems encountered by the male delegates, contributing valuable suggestions in the discussion of boycotting slave-produced goods, and offering solid advice about the composition of the convention's "Declaration of Sentiments and Purposes."[31] Her participation, although cordially and gratefully accepted, did not lead to the inclusion of women when it came time to list the names of members of the American Anti-Slavery Society or to sign the declaration. Thus, talented and aggressive white men held exclusive control of this abolition society from the beginning,

---

[29]Carolyn I. Karcher, *The First Woman of the Republic: A Cultural Biography of Lydia Maria Child* (Durham NC: Duke University Press, 1994) 221.

[30]Anna Davis Hallowell, *James and Lucretia Mott: Life and Letters* (Boston: Houghton Mifflin, 1884) 115–16.

[31]Ibid.

and women continued to be excluded from holding prominent leadership roles in the abolition movement.[32] In its early years, the society, due to its preoccupation with organizational matters and to its apparent obliviousness to the subject of women's roles, avoided dealing with the controversial "woman question." As a result, the society was able to develop its organizational structure and to focus on enrolling members. Within 5 years, 1,346 auxiliaries had been started and the society's membership numbered between 150,000 and 200,000.[33]

The society, however, did encounter serious problems in its early years, including significant opposition from both Southerners and Northerners. Southerners branded society members as radicals and fanatics despite the fact that the society's commitment to non-violence was spelled out clearly in its "Declaration of Sentiments." Angry Southerners often vilified and attacked abolitionists. In Charleston, South Carolina, an angry mob assembled at the post office on 31 August 1835 and hauled away pamphlets that the society had mailed to ministers, elected officials, and newspaper editors. The next day the mob reassembled and hung and burned effigies of Garrison and Arthur Tappan.[34] In the North, community leaders as well as day laborers banded together to defeat the cause of the Anti-Slavery Society. Mobs in New York City, Philadelphia, and Boston showed up at abolition meetings and roughed up participants.[35] This opposition caused dismay and disarray within the abolitionist ranks.[36]

---

[32]James Brewer Stewart, *Holy Warriors: The Abolitionists and American Slavery*, rev. ed., ed. Eric Foner (New York: Hill and Wang, 1996) 52.

[33]Fogel, *Without Consent or Contract*, 271.

[34]Gerda Lerner, *The Grimké Sisters From South Carolina: Pioneers for Woman's Rights and Abolition,* Studies in the Life of Women, ed. Gerda Lerner (New York: Schocken Books, 1971) 93.

[35]Stewart, *Holy Warriors*, 71–72.

[36]Fogel, *Without Consent or Contract*, 271.

Internal dissension also plagued the American Anti-Slavery Society. Within five years of its organization, the society was forced to address the proper role of women. The society's ability to avoid this controversial subject abruptly ended in 1837 when the activities of two Southern women, Sarah and Angelina Grimké, made it impossible for the American Anti-Slavery Society to continue ignoring the "woman question."

The Grimké sisters' movement into the antislavery circle and their endorsement of women's rights occurred over the course of several years. Angelina became the first Grimké sister to support the antislavery cause. In May 1835, she first expressed an interest in abolition, and she soon joined the Philadelphia Female Anti-Slavery Society. By August, Angelina committed herself without reservation to the cause of abolition. As a declaration of her commitment, she wrote a letter to William Lloyd Garrison, proclaiming her full support of the cause of abolition:

> If persecution is the means which God has ordained for the accomplishment of this great end, EMANCIPATION: then, in dependence *upon Him* for strength to bear it, I feel as if I could say, LET IT COME: for it is my deep, solemn, deliberate conviction that *this is a cause worth dying for*. I say so, from what I have seen, and heard, and known, in a land of slavery, where rests the darkness of Egypt, and where is found the sin of Sodom. Yes! LET IT COME—let *us* suffer, rather than that insurrection should arise.[37]

In the letter, Angelina allied herself with the radical wing of abolitionism, the immediatists, by portraying herself as a willing martyr whose self-sacrificing and suffering would save not only slaves and masters but the entire nation.[38]

---

[37]*The Liberator*, 19 September 1835. Emphasis is Angelina's.

[38]Jean Fagan Yellin, *Women and Sisters: The Anti-slavery Feminists in American Culture* (New Haven: Yale University Press, 1989) 32.

Garrison immediately published the letter in *The Liberator,* without Angelina's permission or her knowledge. The letter brought her instant fame among abolitionists and instant disapproval from the Society of Friends and from Sarah.[39] An entry in Sarah's diary reveals her dismay with her younger sister's decision to become involved in the abolition movement: "The suffering which my precious sister has brought upon herself by her connection with the antislavery cause, which has been a sorrow of heart to me, is another proof how dangerous it is to slight the clear convictions of truth.... [S]he listened to the voice of the tempter. Oh! that she may learn obedience by the things that she suffers."[40] Angelina's blatant disregard of her commitment to the Society of Friends and their dismissal of her opposition to radical abolition greatly disturbed Sarah.[41] Involvement in a political cause would most likely result in expulsion from the Quaker meeting, a fate Sarah doubted that Angelina was ready to accept. Sarah also knew of the rebuffs, hostility, and resentment demonstrated toward women who did not confine themselves to their "proper place," and she did not want her sister to be the recipient of such abuse.[42]

Angelina was hurt and disappointed by her sister's reaction and considered Sarah's opposition to be her greatest trial. Yet, despite Sarah's continued condemnation, Angelina held firm.[43] She believed

---

[39]Gerda Lerner, *The Feminist Thought of Sarah Grimké* (New York/Oxford: Oxford University Press, 1998) 12.

[40]Sarah Grimké, diary, 25 September 1835, 101. Weld-Grimké Collection, William L. Clements Library, University of Michigan, Ann Arbor.

[41]Alma Lutz, *Crusade for Freedom: Women of the Antislavery Movement* (Boston: Beacon Press, 1968) 91.

[42]Judith Nies, *Seven Women: Portraits from the American Radical Tradition* (New York: Viking Press, 1977) 19.

[43]Angelina also was dismayed by the continued opposition to the abolition cause by other members of her family, especially her mother. A few months after the publication of Angelina's letter in *The Liberator,* her mother wrote both Angelina and Sarah informing them that she had written her will. Angelina immediately wrote her mother in attempt to convert

that abolition was now her calling, and she refused to retreat from what she considered to be her obligation to those held in bondage.[44]

In the summer of 1836, Angelina found a way to contribute further to the cause of abolition. She declared: "God has shown me what I can do; I can write an appeal to Southern women, one which, thus inspired, will touch their hearts, and lead them to use their influence with their husbands and brothers. I will speak to them in such tones that they must hear me, and through me, the voice of justice and humanity."[45] The American Anti-Slavery Society published her thirty-six-page pamphlet, titled *Appeal to the Christian Women of the South.*[46] The pamphlet, which sold for six-and-a half cents a copy, circulated widely in the North. In the South, outraged Southern postmasters often publicly burned it.[47]

Within a few months of the publication of Angelina's *Appeal*, Sarah, now forty-three years old, changed her mind and joined Angelina in supporting the antislavery cause. Her transformation into an ardent abolitionist may be attributed to several factors. First,

---

Mrs. Grimké to abolitionism. Knowing that her mother's conversion was unlikely, Angelina begged her mother to bequeath all the Grimké slaves to Sarah and herself so that these slaves eventually might be freed. Angelina was persuasive, and when Mrs. Grimké died in 1839, she willed her slaves to Sarah, Angelina, and a third sister, Anna Frost. They received two adult slaves and several young children who were freed immediately. Sarah and Angelina assisted them financially and even offered to house them if they decided to move to the North. See Janet Stevenson, "A Family Divided," *American Heritage* 18/1 (April 1967): 84.

[44]Catherine H. Birney, *Sarah and Angelina Grimké: The First American Women Advocates of Abolition and Woman's Rights* (Lee and Shephard, 1885; reprint, Westport CT: Greenwood Press, 1969) 131, 142.

[45]Angelina Grimké, diary, quoted in Birney, *Sarah and Angelina Grimké*, 138.

[46]For a discussion of Angelina's decision to write the *Appeal* and for an analysis of its content, see Stephan Howard Browne, *Angelina Grimké: Rhetoric, Identity and Radical Imagination, Rhetoric and Public Affairs Series* (East Lansing: Michigan State University Press, 1999) 55–82.

[47]Stevenson, "A Family Divided," 84.

her estrangement with Angelina caused by their disagreement about involvement in abolition deeply upset Sarah. In a letter to Jane Smith, Sarah wrote, "Perhaps the Lord may be pleased to cast our lot somewhere together. If so, I feel as if I could ask no more in this world."[48]

Second, Sarah's own conflict over the issue of her ministry contributed to her departure from the Society of Friends. Her tolerance of the Quaker leadership's opposition finally ran out after Jonathan Edwards, a Quaker elder, openly criticized her on 3 August 1836 during a worship service at a Fourth and Arch Street meeting.[49] Edwards's public silencing of Sarah's speaking, which was a breach of Quaker practice, provided her with a release from her Quaker commitment.[50] She then determined to quit the Society of Friends, and she sought to ease her disappointment by immersing herself in the abolition cause.

Third, and most importantly, Sarah concluded that her participation in the antislavery movement was the will of God. She based her commitment to the cause on religious convictions. For Sarah, the true test of whether she and Angelina should support abolition was whether their support was in accordance with God's holy will, and by the end of the summer of 1836, Sarah concluded that working to end slavery was indeed God's will for her.[51]

Just a few months before, the sisters, because of their disagreements with the Quakers, felt they could no longer accept the hospitality of Catherine Morris, and they had made other housing arrangements. Angelina went to Shrewsbury, New Jersey, and stayed with her friend Margaret Parker. Sarah moved to Burlington, New Jersey, and became the houseguest of Orthodox Quaker

---

[48]Sarah Grimké to Jane Smith, n.d., in Birney, *Sarah and Angelina Grimké*, 139.

[49]Sarah Grimké to Theodore Weld, 10 March 1837, in Barnes and Dumond, *Letters of Theodore Dwight Weld*, 1:373.

[50]Birney, *Sarah and Angelina Grimké*, 143–44.

[51]Grimké, diary, 19 July 1836, 25.

friends, Peter and Abigail Barker.[52] While living with the Barkers, Sarah made her final decision to leave the Society of Friends, and she wrote Angelina to tell her of this news. Sarah's change of heart concerning the abolition movement thrilled her younger sister. Upon receiving Sarah's letter, Angelina wrote this reply to her sister: "I cannot be too thankful for the change in thy feelings with regard to the A S Society & feel no desire at all to blame thee for former opposition, believing as I do that it was permitted in order to drive me closer to my Savior & into a deeper examination as to the ground upon which I was standing."[53]

Once her decision was made, Sarah withstood the disapproving attitudes and threats of disownment by the Quakers. She knew that the "Friends were aware they would be in an awkward position for disowning us for an activity in which they themselves had been engaged and which was interwoven with their principles."[54] Yet she also knew that whatever the Quaker meeting chose to do, she had now cast her lot with Angelina and had committed herself to the antislavery cause. This decision to leave the Quakers was a turning point in Sarah's life, one that was instigated by her beloved sister Angelina.[55] To this point in their lives, Sarah had been the leader. She ensured that Angelina had a more positive and carefree childhood than she herself had known. She had converted Angelina to Quakerism. But now it was Angelina who led the way for the sisters. Angelina's decision to move into the antislavery movement provided for Sarah a practical outlet for her long-held antislavery convictions.

---

[52]Lerner, *The Grimké Sisters From South Carolina*, 107.

[53]Angelina E. Grimké to Sarah M. Grimké, *The Public Years of Sarah and Angelina Grimké: Selected Writings, 1835–1839*, ed. Larry Ceplair (New York: Columbia University Press, 1989) 35.

[54]Sarah Grimké, "Letter on the Subject of Prejudice Against Colour Amongst the Society of Friends in the United States," 24–25, Sarah Grimké Papers, Boston Public Library, Boston, MA.

[55]Lerner, *The Feminist Thought of Sarah Grimké*, 13.

In October 1836, the Grimké sisters traveled to New York and stayed in the home of Abraham and Abby Cox. After consulting with Elizur Wright, the corresponding secretary of the American Anti-Slavery Society, the Grimkés planned their future. They determined to form a National Female Anti-Slavery Society. Female Anti-Slavery Societies already existed in cities such as Philadelphia, Boston, and New York. Under the direction of Wright, the Grimké sisters along with Abby Cox determined that a national female society must be formed.[56]

In the preceding years as more women joined the abolition crusade, they began to see the need to establish separate female antislavery societies. The women involved in these female societies worked to support the men's organizations and focused attention on the female victims of slavery. The formation of these separate female societies throughout the 1830s may be attributed to several factors. First, by establishing their own societies, women could focus their efforts on issues they felt to be pertinent, such as domestic difficulties. Female societies often addressed problems that proved to be especially harmful to the lives of women and children, including drunkenness, poverty, and prostitution. The female abolitionists, however, did not merely address the problems of white women and children; they championed the cause of slave women and children. The female antislavery societies denounced the sexual exploitation and inhuman treatment to which female slaves were subjected. The female abolitionists asserted that this aspect of slavery was not only cruel and humiliating but that it tended to destroy the ties that women valued above all others—the bonds of family.[57]

Second, these separate societies provided women with a sense of sisterhood. The societies allowed women to meet together on a regular basis and to unify their efforts in ending moral "evils."

[56]Melder, *Beginning of Sisterhood*, 64–67. See also Lerner, *The Grimké Sisters From South Carolina*, 144, 147.

[57]Melder, *Beginning of Sisterhood*, 57–58. See also Bass, "The Best Hopes of the Sexes," 44, 46–47.

Finally, women gained the opportunity to hold positions of leadership and to experience some sense of power and control within these separate organizations.[58] In the early days of the abolition movement, women joined the male-led societies, and as they worked within these societies, many of these women grew dissatisfied with the secondary roles they were given. They questioned their "proper" roles within the movement and pushed for greater leadership. A number of women soon began to work for and to demand full equality within the abolition movement, and they found that forming separate female societies was one way they could assure that they would have a voice and be full participants in the work of abolition.

In late 1836, the Grimké sisters recognized the importance of these female antislavery society, and they concluded that the local female antislavery societies must be united, and a national organization must be founded. The Grimkés determined to establish such an organization. They also decided that they would serve as agents of this new society and travel especially in New England, speaking to groups of women and distributing tracts, to promote the society's cause.[59] To prepare themselves for such a task, the Grimkés attended the Agents' Convention of the American Anti-Slavery Society held 8–27 November 1836. Angelina was the only woman to be invited to join the forty men attending this training

---

[58]See Bass, "The Best Hopes of the Sexes," 43 and Melder, *Beginning of Sisterhood*, 40–41. See also Aileen S. Kraditor, *Means and Ends in American Abolitionism: Garrison and His Critics on Strategy and Tactics, 1834–1850* (New York: Pantheon Books, 1967) 41.

[59]Both the American Anti-Slavery Society and the National Female Anti-Slavery Society published the tracts that the Grimké sisters distributed. Most likely the sisters even distributed Angelina's own pamphlets *Appeal to the Christian Women of the South* (1836) and *Appeal to the Women of the Nominally Free States* (1837). These and the other pamphlets they sold contained the call for women to involve themselves in the fight against slavery and justified such involvement as women's duty. See Melder, *Beginning of Sisterhood*, 78–80.

convention, but Sarah accompanied her sister to every meeting, and Sarah's presence was cordially accepted.[60]

At the meetings of the Agents' Convention, the Grimké sisters, along with other recruits often referred to as "The Seventy,"[61] were given intensive training in the method and theory of abolition work. They refined their arguments against slavery, rehearsed their responses to questions and confrontations, and laid a foundation for a system of encouragement and support.[62] The sisters also met for the first time many of the outstanding abolitionists of the day—William Lloyd Garrison, Henry Stanton, Lewis and Arthur Tappan, and Theodore Dwight Weld. The intelligence and dedication of Sarah and Angelina so impressed the experienced abolition leaders that they voted to invite the Grimkés "to speak whenever they think proper, and to state such facts respecting slavery as they may choose."[63]

Sarah took advantage of the unusual opportunity and at one of the meetings spoke boldly of her firsthand knowledge of slavery.[64] Although no transcripts of Sarah's speeches have survived, the content most likely resembled a personal narrative she later wrote for Theodore Weld's *American Slavery as It Is: Testimony of a Thousand Witnesses*. She began that narrative by stating:

---

[60]Larry Ceplair, ed., *The Public Years of Sarah and Angelina Grimké: Selected Writings, 1835–1839* (New York: Columbia University Press, 1989) 23.

[61]The use of the name, "The Seventy," was a reference to Luke 10:1: "After this the Lord appointed other seventy also, and sent them two and two before his face to every city and place, whither he himself would come." (KJV)

[62]Bass, "The Best Hopes of the Sexes," 105.

[63]William Lloyd Garrison to Helen E. Garrison, 22 November 1836 in *The Letters of William Lloyd Garrison, eds. Walter M. Merrill and Louis Ruchames* (Cambridge MA: Belknap Press, 1971) A House Dividing Against Itself, 1836–1840, ed. Louis Ruchames, 2:185.

[64]Wendall P. Garrison and Francis J. Garrison, *William Lloyd Garrison: 1805–1879: The Story of His Life Told by His Children* (New York: The Century Co., 1885–1889) 2:117.

As I left my native state on account of slavery, and deserted the home of my fathers to escape the sound of the lash and the shrieks of tortured victims, I would gladly bury in oblivion the recollection of those scenes with which I have been familiar; but this may not, cannot be; they come over my memory like gory spectres, and implore me with resistless power, in the name of a God of mercy, in the name of a crucified Savior, in the name of humanity; for the sake of the slaveholder, as well as the slave, to bear witness to the horrors of the southern prison houses. I feel impelled by a sacred sense of duty, by my obligation to my country, by sympathy for the bleeding victims of tyranny and lust, to give my testimony respecting the system of American slavery,—to detail a few facts, most of which came under my personal observation.[65]

Sarah continued her narrative by providing detailed descriptions of the beatings, starvation, and tortuous death imposed on rebellious slaves. She presumably shared this type of information with the agents of American Anti-Slavery Society and continued to share it in her role as an agent of the Female Anti-Slavery Society.

Shortly after the exhilarating and exhausting experience of the Agents' Convention of 1836, the Grimké sisters set out, under the auspices of the newly formed Female Anti-Slavery Society, to present a series of "parlor talks" in the New York City area. These meetings were to be held in private homes for the purpose of informing and involving women in the cause of abolition. It soon became obvious, however, that no parlor in the city could hold all the women who wanted to attend these meetings. A Baptist clergyman, the Reverend Dunbar, solved the dilemma by offering

[65]Sarah M. Grimké, "Narrative and Testimony of Sarah M. Grimké," in *American Slavery as It Is: Testimony of a Thousand Witnesses*, ed. by Theodore Weld (New York: American Anti-Slavery Society, 1839; reprint, New York: Arno Press, 1968) 22.

the Female Society the use of a session room in his church. Despite the prejudices against women speaking in public places, the Grimkés agreed to the arrangement.

Some within the abolition movement opposed the decision to hold abolition meetings in a public place. The prominent New York abolitionist, Gerrit Smith, advised the sisters to cancel the meetings because these meetings would be perceived as "Fanny Wright meetings" and would do more harm than good.[66] The opposition caused the sisters to reconsider their decision to speak out publicly against slavery. Both questioned whether they should proceed in the face of such antagonism. Yet, due to the encouragement and strong insistence of Theodore Weld, they carried out their endeavor.

The Grimkés' "parlor talks" began in December 1836 and were held every Friday afternoon at three o'clock. More than three hundred women attended the first meeting. It began with a prayer led by Henry Ludlow, a Presbyterian minister and committed abolitionist, followed by a warm welcome from the Reverend Dunbar. The two men then left the church building, and the two sisters took over the meeting. Angelina spoke first for about forty minutes, followed by Sarah. According to Angelina, Sarah "did her part better than I."[67] In her speech, Sarah discussed the laws of the slave states, read testimony from Southerners attesting to the evils of slavery, and answered questions. Her first attempt at public

---

[66]Ceplair, *The Public Years of Sarah and Angelina Grimké*, 88. Fanny Wright was a Scotswoman who visited the United States in 1820. Appalled by the institution of slavery, she sought to implement a plan for the abolition of slaves. Her plan included the establishment of a model community at Nashoba, Tennessee, in which blacks lived and worked together. The model community failed, partly because of a sexual scandal connected to it and to her. Her unorthodox abolition activities and her outspokenness resulted in her being ostracized by polite society. She was often referred to as the "notorious Fanny Wright," and any woman who dared to speak in public or to accept a leadership role was soon labeled with the scandalous title of "Fanny Wright."

[67]Ibid., 89.

speaking was clearly a success. The women present unanimously voted to continue the meetings.

The lectures continued until February 1837, eventually moving from the session room to the church sanctuary in order to accommodate the growing number of women attending the meetings. The popularity of the Grimkés most likely can be attributed to their status as former slaveholders. Their descriptions of slavery had an authenticity that could only be surpassed by those of former slaves, and the intense devotion of these two women to their cause won many members of their audiences to the abolition movement. That they happened to be women increased their appeal to a curious public.[68]

Inevitably, men began to attend these meetings, sitting at the back of the lecture halls or in the doorways. The first time men attended a meeting was in late January 1837. Angelina described the event in a letter to her friend Jane Smith: "We had one male auditor, who refused to go out when H G L[udlow] told him it was exclusively for ladys [*sic*] & so there he sat & somehow I did not feel his presence at all embarrassing & went on just as tho' [*sic*] he was not there. Some one said he took notes, & I think he was a Southern spy & shall not be at all surprized [*sic*] if he published us in some Southern paper, for we hav[e] heard of him here."[69] The man was not a spy, but only the first of many men who desired to hear these two women abolitionists speak.

For the Grimké sisters, their newfound careers as antislavery agents satisfied both their lifelong need to be productive as well as their religious drive to bring about reform. For Sarah, the cause of abolition became an increasingly vital part of her life. In a letter to Jane Smith, she declared, "I would not give up my abolition feelings for anything I know. They are intertwined with my Christianity.

---

[68]Kraditor, *Means and Ends in American Abolitionism*, 42.

[69]Angelina E. Grimké to Jane Smith, 4 February 1837, in Ceplair, *The Public Years of Sarah and Angelina Grimké*, 116.

They have given a new spring to my existence."[70] Her work as an abolitionist seemed to provide the fulfillment for which she had searched since childhood.

Sarah's commitment to the cause of abolition was not just a commitment to end slavery but a commitment to end racial prejudice.[71] In her lectures, Sarah often charged her listeners to work, as she did, for racial equality. During the months she spent in New York, Sarah and Angelina taught Sunday school classes to black children and visited the their homes.[72] Sarah also helped organize an association for the benefit of black orphans. In late 1836, she wrote a critique of the blatant racial prejudice found in the Society of Friends.[73] Apparently, she showed this critique to Theodore Weld who advised her not to publish it.

It was also in late 1836 that Sarah produced her *Epistle to the Clergy of the Southern States,* in which she appealed to Southern clergymen to take a stand against slavery. Sarah also offered an explanation of the moral, legal, and biblical arguments used by abolitionists.[74] Most of the arguments set forth in the *Epistle to the Clergy* were bolstered by Sarah's citing of scriptural mandates. To support her assertion that slavery was a crime because it turned human beings into objects, she quoted Genesis 1:26. According to Sarah, this verse—"And God said, Let us make man in our image,

---

[70]Sarah Grimké to Jane Smith, n.d., in Birney, *Sarah and Angelina Grimké*, 165.

[71]Frank G. Kirkpatrick, "From Shackles to Liberation: Religion, the Grimké Sister and Dissent," in *Women, Religion, and Social Change,* ed. Yvonne Yazbeck and Ellison Banks Findly (Albany: State University of New York Press, 1985) 450.

[72] Lerner, *The Grimké Sisters From South Carolina,* 158.

[73]Three years later, in 1839, Sarah circulated another critique of the Society of Friends' attitudes on racial relations titled "Letters on the Subject of Prejudice Amongst the Society of Friends in the United States." Parts of this letter appeared in the British pamphlet *Society of Friends: Their Views of the Anti-Slavery Question, and Treatment of the People of Colour.* See Lerner, *The Grimké Sisters From South Carolina,* 256.

[74]Lerner, *The Grimké Sisters From South Carolina,* 155.

after our likeness"—proved that God not only created all human being in his image but that God expected all persons to be treated with respect. Sarah then cited Genesis 9:3 as evidence that God intended humans to have dominion over animals and nature but not over other human beings. Genesis 9:3 reads: "Every moving thing that liveth shall be meat for you; even as the green herb have I given you all things." Sarah believed that these verses in Genesis demonstrated that slavery was not part of God's intention because slavery allowed persons made in the image of God to be treated like animals, thereby destroying the unique image of God within those persons.[75] She wrote, "We are fighting against God's unchangeable decree by depriving this rational and immortal being of those inalienable rights which have been conferred upon him."[76]

In the *Epistle to the Clergy of the Southern States*, Sarah also denounced of the use of Genesis 9:24–27 to defend slavery.[77] These slaveholders interpreted these verses to mean that Noah cursed Ham and that Africans, as Ham's descendents, were also cursed. Therefore, according to these slaveholders, the enslavement of Africans was "in accordance with the declaration of Jehovah."[78] Sarah concluded that if the verses were in fact referring to a curse, it should not be understood not as a curse on Ham but as a curse on the Canaanites.[79] But Sarah believed that these verses in Genesis were not truly a curse at all but rather were a prophecy, for the

---

[75]Lerner, *The Feminist Thought of Sarah Grimké*, 14.

[76]Sarah M. Grimké, "An Epistle to the Clergy of the Southern States," in Ceplair, *The Public Years of Sarah and Angelina Grimké*, 92.

[77]Genesis 9:24–27 reads: "And Noah awoke from his wine, and knew what his younger son had done unto him. And he said, 'Cursed be Canaan; a servant of servants shall he be unto his brethren.' And he said, 'Blessed be the Lord God of Shem; and Canaan shall be his servant. God shall enlarge Japheth and he shall dwell in the tents of Shem; and Canaan shall be his servant.'"

[78]Sarah M. Grimké, "An Epistle to the Clergy of the Southern States," in Ceplair, *The Public Years of Sarah and Angelina Grimké*, 99.

[79]Ibid.

writer of Genesis was offering a prophetic word about what happens among human beings after their fall.[80]

The writing of the *Epistle to the Clergy* along with her lecturing and her personal involvement with free blacks brought Sarah satisfaction and fulfillment. She believed that she finally had found her calling in life.

Near the end of February 1837, the Grimké sisters began to expand their lecture circuit. They traveled to New Jersey, holding meetings and enlisting women in the National Female Anti-Slavery Society. They then visited their "home" city of Philadelphia, and during one of their lectures there, a mob gathered and rioted outside the lecture hall. Later that night that building was burned down. Despite the presence of a mob and the threat of violence, the Grimkés remained calm. Their courage and perseverance inspired their audiences.[81]

While visiting in Philadelphia, the Grimké sisters attended worship at the Fourth and Arch Street Meeting, the Quaker congregation of which they had been members for so many years. Their presence stirred up quite a controversy because Sarah and Angelina sat on the "Negro pew." While members at Fourth and Arch Street, the sisters had developed friendships with many freed blacks, including Grace and Sarah Douglass. This return trip to their own meeting house convinced the Grimkés that racism had infected this Quaker congregation, and they sat on the "Negro pew" to demonstrate their displeasure with the meeting house and to show their support for and friendship with all black people.[82] Following this worship service, Sarah and Angelina were reprimanded for their

---

[80]Lerner, *The Feminist Thought of Sarah Grimké*, 14.

[81]Glenna Matthews, *The Rise of Public Woman: Woman's Power and Woman's Place in the United States, 1630–1970* (New York/Oxford: Oxford University Press, 1992) 113.

[82]Carolyn Williams, "Racial Prejudice and Women's Rights," in *The Abolitionist Sisterhood: Women's Political Culture in Antebellum America*, ed. Jean Fagan Yellin and John C. Van Horne (Ithaca/London: Cornell University Press, 1994) 168.

action and for attending a Presbyterian church in New York. The Quaker leaders of the Fourth and Arch Street Meeting urged the Grimkés to resign their membership in the Society of Friends in order to avoid the embarrassment of being disowned. The sisters refused. They insisted that they still held to the great principles of the Quaker faith, and they placed the responsibility of their leaving the Society of Friends upon the Quakers themselves. Sarah wrote, "Upon Friends, not upon us must rest the responsibility of depriving us of the right of membership."[83] The Elders of the Society of Friends, however, failed to carry out their threat of disownment, and the Grimkés continued to consider themselves to be Quakers.

After several more months of touring, the sisters attended the Anti-Slavery Convention of American Women in New York City. Seventy-one women were present at this May 1837 organizational effort of American female abolitionists. The convention assembled in response to the "gag rule" that had been passed by the United States House of Representatives on 26 May 1836. The rule stated that "all petitions relating...to the subject of slavery or the abolition of slavery, shall, without being either printed or referred, be laid upon the table, and...no further action whatever shall be had thereon."[84] The women saw the action by Congress as a threat to what was perhaps the most vital means abolitionists had in attempting to further their cause. They decided to mount a national campaign in which they would flood Congress with petitions. The American Anti-Slavery Society, meeting simultaneously, also adopted the program and appointed a committee to oversee the national petition campaign that was expected to rely heavily on women volunteers.[85]

---

[83]Grimké, "Letter on Prejudice Against Colour," 29–30.

[84] The Proceedings, Anti-Slavery Convention of American Women, Held by Adjournment from the 9th to the 12th May 1837 (New York: W. S. Dorr, 1837) quoted in Gilbert Hobbs Barnes, *The Antislavery Impulse: 1830–1844* (New York: D. Appleton-Century Company, 1933) 110.

[85]Women had proven to be more successful in petition campaigns. In April 1837, *The Liberator* reported that in New England alone female

With such a monumental task before them, the women of the Anti-Slavery Convention set up an organizational structure to guarantee their success. Sarah was elected as one of six vice presidents, and Angelina became one of four secretaries. The convention also appointed the Grimké sisters to committees. Sarah was assigned to the committee in charge of preparing an "Address to Free Coloured Americans." Angelina was assigned to a committee whose task was to write "An Appeal to Women of the Nominally Free States." Angelina also served on a committee that was charged with writing a letter to John Quincy Adams, a former President of the United States (1825–1829) and a current member of the House of Representatives (1831–1848).[86] Adams had worked to revoke the "gag rule" of May 1836 because he believed the rule violated the First Amendment. He also called for women to have the right to mount petition campaigns. In the letter written by Angelina's committee, the women praised Adams for his efforts on their behalf, but the women condemned his lack of commitment to ending slavery in the District of Columbia.[87]

The Grimkés provided further leadership at the convention by submitting ten resolutions concerning fugitive slaves, the right of petition, the need for open and equal education, and a protest against racial prejudice. Angelina submitted a resolution that stated: "The existence of an unnatural prejudice against our colored population is one of the chief pillars of American slavery;" therefore, we must "act out the principles of Christian equality by associating with

---

petitions outnumbered male petitions by a two to one ratio. See Bass, "The Best Hopes of the Sexes," 66.

[86]"John Quincy Adams Defends the Right of Petition," *The Antislavery Argument*, ed. William H. Pease and Jane H. Pease (Indianapolis: Bobbs-Merrill Co., 1965) 260–72.

[87]Ruth Bogin and Jean Fagan Yellin, Introduction to *The Abolitionist Sisterhood: Women's Political Culture in Antebellum America*, ed. Jean Fagan Yellin and John C. Van Horne (Ithaca/ London: Cornell University Press, 1994) 13–14.

them."[88] Sarah offered a resolution that condemned "northern men and women, who marry slaveholders," and she wrote a resolution that called on women "as moral and responsible beings" to discuss the subject of slavery.[89] Another of Sarah's proposed resolution called on American mothers to "educate their children in the principles of peace, and special abhorrence of that warfare, which gives aid to the oppressor against the oppressed."[90] Eight of the ten Grimké proposed resolutions gained immediate and unanimous support from the convention.

A final contribution made by the Grimkés at this convention was their encouragement of the attendance of this meeting by black women. As a result of their encouragement, several black women were present and played major roles. Grace Douglass was elected as a vice president, and Sarah Douglass was asked to serve on the committee assigned to the preparation of "Address to Free Coloured Americans."[91] Speeches by the Grimké sisters at this convention reveal their growing commitment to not only the abolition of slavery but to the abolition of racism.

After the convention, the Grimké sisters moved on to New England. In Massachusetts, they received a warm welcome from the Boston Female Anti-Slavery Society. The positive reception was due, in part, to a letter that its leading member, Maria Chapman, wrote in support of the Grimkés' tour. Encouraged by their reception, the sisters continued their abolition work. They attended parlor meetings in the homes of leading abolitionists and spoke to

---

[88]The Proceedings, Anti-Slavery Convention of American Women, Held by Adjournment from the 9th to the 12th May 1837 (New York: W. S. Dorr, 1837); quoted in Lerner, *The Feminist Thought of Sarah Grimké*, 18.

[89]Ibid.

[90]The Proceedings, Anti-Slavery Convention of American Women, Held by Adjournment from the 9th to the 12th May 1837 (New York: W. S. Dorr, 1837) 8–12; quoted by Bogin and Yellin, Introduction to *The Abolitionist Sisterhood*, 15.

[91]Williams, "Racial Prejudice and Women's Rights," 168–69.

large public meetings of the Boston Female Anti-Slavery Society. Sarah soon sensed a measure of freedom in Boston that she had never experienced before. In a letter to Weld, she proclaimed, "I have been truly refreshed by mingling with the abolitionists of Boston and its vicinity; there is some elasticity in this atmosphere; I feel as if I was helped, strengthened, invigorated."[92]

As a result of the relaxed atmosphere in Boston, the sisters began to express their thoughts on women's rights in private meetings with like-minded abolitionists. The support that the Grimkés received from prominent female abolitionists in Boston encouraged them to share these thoughts on women's rights in their public meetings. Speaking before an audience composed of 300 women, Sarah and Angelina proclaimed that women, instead of being embarrassed or restrained in the presence of men, should recognize that they have been charged with the responsibility of initiating and implementing reform.[93]

The notoriety of the Grimkés increased due to their new stance on women's rights, and they began attracting larger crowds composed of both women and men. Sarah and Angelina left Boston and continued on their lecturing tour, visiting the Massachusetts counties of Essex, Middlesex, and Worcester. Their speeches drew larger audiences. The Grimkés spoke to nearly 300 women and men in Roxbury.[94] In Lynn, Massachusetts, they encountered their first "mixed" audience of significant size. On the evening of 21 June 1837, over 1,000 men and women attended one of the Grimkés' meetings. With only 600 seats available, many persons were turned away, and some stood around the doors and windows in order to hear. Speaking before men had become a routine occurrence for the sisters. In a letter to Gerrit Smith, Sarah summed up the experience

---

[92]Sarah Grimké to Theodore Weld, 11 June 1837, in Barnes and Dumond, *Letters of Theodore Dwight Weld*, 1:401.

[93]Lerner, *The Grimké Sisters From South Carolina*, 166.

[94]Debra Gold Hansen, *Strained Sisterhood: Gender and Class in the Boston Female Anti-Slavery Society* (Amherst: The University of Massachusetts Press, 1993) 22.

of expanding their audiences to include men: "One brother wanted
to come and another thought he had a right and now the door is
wide open. Whosoever will come and hear our testimony may
come."[95] Their audiences grew even more as the tour continued. In
Lowell, they lectured to over 1,500 people, and their 3 lectures in
Salem drew 2,400 listeners.[96] Despite the popularity of the Grimké
sisters, their public speeches and the presence of men at these
speeches stirred up much controversy. The clergy, male
abolitionists, and even women criticized the Grimkés.

The first public criticism of the Grimké sisters' abolition work
came in early February 1837, when the New Haven *Religious
Intelligencer* published a letter signed by a man identified only as
"Clarkson." The letter argued that Northerners did not need the
sisters to "undeceive" them about the "wickedness, cruelty and
oppression of slavery" because Northerners had understood the
injustices of slavery for forty or fifty years. "Clarkson" challenged
the sisters to present "definite practicable means" by which
Northerners could put an end to slavery in the South.[97]

The Grimkés encountered more criticism as they continued to
tour the New England states. The most damaging criticism came
from the clergy of Massachusetts. In mid-1837, Congregational
ministers belonging to the General Association of Massachusetts
authorized the Reverend Nehemiah Adams of Boston to write a
response to the abolition movement and to the presence of female
leaders in that movement. His work, "Pastoral Letter of the General
Association of Massachusetts to the Congregational Churches under
their Care," was read from pulpits and finally published in the 12
July edition of the *New England Spectator*. The letter spoke directly
to the question of a woman's proper sphere of activity.

Although the letter did not mention the sisters specifically,
Adams clearly had them in mind as he wrote. He denounced women

---

[95]Sarah Grimké to Gerrit Smith, 28 June 1837, in Ibid., 1:410.

[96]Hansen, *Strained Sisterhood*, 22.

[97]"Clarkson" letter, in Barnes and Dumond, *Letters of Theodore Dwight
Weld*, 1:365–66.

who assumed "the place and tone of man as a public reformer." He also stated that "the appropriate duties and influence of women are clearly stated in the New Testament. Those duties and that influence are unobtrusive and private."[98]

Criticism directed at the Grimkés, however, did not come solely from persons outside the abolition movement. Indeed, the Grimkés' position as public spokeswomen for the cause of abolition stirred up much controversy within the Anti-Slavery Society. Staunch male abolitionists and even some of the women abolitionists strongly opposed the direction that the Grimkés had chosen to take in their abolition efforts.

From the beginning of their association with the American Anti-Slavery Society, the Grimkés received endorsements from many of its pivotal leaders. Men such as Garrison supported the sisters' work. His commitment to promote the rights of women especially comforted and encouraged Sarah and Angelina. In a letter dated 27 August 1837, Sarah wrote of Garrison: "It has cheered my spirit to find that he unites fully with us on the subject of the rights of woman."[99]

Yet many of the male members of the Society opposed the Grimkés' decision to address the issue of women's rights. These men objected to what they perceived as the sisters' abandonment or dilution of abolition for the cause of women's rights. Even Theodore Weld, one of the Grimkés' staunchest supporters and Angelina's future husband, sought to convince the sisters to discontinue their outspokenness on the woman issue. In August 1837, he wrote to the sisters:

I advocate now, that woman in EVERY *particular* shares equally with man rights and responsibilities. Now I

---

[98]"Pastoral Letter: The General Association of Massachusetts to the Churches Under Their Care," in Ceplair, *The Public Years of Sarah and Angelina Grimké*, 211.

[99]Sarah Grimké to Henry C. Wright, 27 August 1837, in Barnes and Dumond, *Letters of Theodore Dwight Weld*, 1:438

have made this statement of my *creed* on this point to show
you that we *fully agree in principle*.... Now notwithstanding
this, I do most deeply regret that you have begun a series of
articles in the Papers on the rights of woman. Why, my dear
sisters, the best possible advocacy which you can make is
just what you are making day by day. Thousands hear you
every week who have all their lives held that woman must
not speak in public. Such a practical refutation of the dogma
as your speaking furnishes has already converted
multitudes.... [Y]ou are *Southerners,* have been
slaveholders; your dearest friends are all in the sin and
shame and peril. All these things give you great access to
northern mind, great *sway* over it. You can do ten times as
much on the subject of *slavery* as Mrs. Child or Mrs.
Chapman. Why? Not because your powers are superior to
theirs, but because you are *southerners*. You can do more at
convincing the north than twenty *northern* females, tho' [*sic*]
they could speak as well as you. Now this peculiar advantage
you *lose* the moment you take *another* subject. You come
down from your vantage ground. *Any* women of your powers
will produce as much effect as you do on the north in
advocating the rights of *free* women (I mean in
contradistinction to *slave* women). Further, almost any other
woman of your capacities and station could produce a
greater effect on the public mind on that subject than *you*,
because you are quakers and that is a *quaker* doctrine, and
all sects are expected to try for proselytes.... Now can't you
leave the *lesser* work to others who can do it *better* than you,
and devote, consecrate your whole bodies, souls and spirits
to the *greater* work which you can do far better and to far
better purpose than any body else. Again, the abolition
question is most powerfully preparative and introductory to

the *other* question. By pushing the former with all our might we are most effectually advancing the latter.[100]

Weld's letter greatly disturbed the Grimkés because he had been their encourager and their champion. Now they feared that he would abandon them.

Another male abolitionist who objected to the Grimkés' defense of women's rights was John Greenleaf Whittier. Whittier privately tried to convince the sisters to discontinue their discussions on the rights of women and to focus solely on abolition. In August 1837, he wrote the sisters and asked them:

> Does it not *look*, dear sisters, like abandoning in some degree the cause of the poor and miserable slave, sighing from the cotton plantation of the Mississippi, and whose cries and groans are forever sounding in our ears, for the purpose of arguing and disputing about some trifling oppression, political or social, which we may ourselves suffer? Is it not forgetting the great and dreadful wrongs of the slave in a selfish crusade against some paltry grievance of our own? Forgive me if I have stated the case too strongly. I would not for the world interfere with you in matters of conscientious duty, but I wish you would weigh candidly the whole subject, and see if it does not seem an abandonment to your first love. Oh let us try to forget everything but our duty to God and our fellow beings; to dethrone the selfish principle, and to strive to win over the hard heart of the oppressor by truth kindly spoken.[101]

Like Weld, Whittier supported the principle of women's rights but strongly believed that it held a secondary position to the cause

---

[100]Theodore Weld to Sarah and Angelina Grimké, 15 August 1837, in Ibid., 1:425–26.

[101]John Greenleaf Whittier to Sarah and Angelina Grimké, 14 August 1837 in Ibid., 1:424.

of abolition. Thus, he appealed to the sisters not to give up completely on the ideal of winning equal rights for women but to delay their cause until the slavery issue was solved.

Other male leaders in the abolition movement objected to the Grimkés speaking out on women's rights not because they believed that the woman issue might possibly overshadow the slavery issue. Instead, they opposed women's rights altogether. Lewis Tappan, James Birney, and Amos Phelps sought to silence the Grimkés on the grounds that the participation of women in men's affairs was "a moral wrong—a thing forbidden alike by the word of God, the dictates of right reason, the voice of wisdom, and the modesty of unperverted nature."[102]

Many abolitionist women also were not open to the Grimkés' emphasis on women's rights. These women felt comfortable working within separate female organizations and believed that their efforts in gathering petitions and raising money were beneficial to the cause. Yet they were content to leave the public speaking and the decision-making to men. The Grimkés' actions, however, forced these women to struggle with the "woman question." When confronted with this moral dilemma, Juliana Tappan, the eldest daughter of the longtime abolitionist leader Lewis Tappan, expressed doubts about women assuming public roles in the abolition movement. She wrote:

> Is it not very difficult to draw the boundary line? On the one hand, we are in danger of servile submission to the opinions of the other sex, & on the other hand, in perhaps equal danger of losing that modesty, & instinctive delicacy of feeling, which our Creator has given as a safeguard to protect us from dangers, to which on account of our weakness, we are continually exposed. How difficult it is to

---

[102]From the Constitution of the Massachusetts Abolition Society, the anti-Garrison organization, quoted in Barnes, *The Antislavery Impulse*, 159.

ascertain what duty is, when we consult the stereotyped opinions of the world.[103]

Tappan's perplexity most likely represented the feelings of many women who were forced for the first time to grapple with questions concerning the role of women in society.

The criticism of some of the clergy, male abolition leaders, and fellow women workers prompted Sarah and Angelina to write numerous articles, letters, and essays. Their first response was a reply to "Clarkson," in which they answered his challenge by producing a detailed program for ending slavery in the South. Their reply, published in *Friend of Man* in early April 1837, included the following suggestions: Northerners should (1) petition Congress to abolish slavery and the slave trade in the District of Columbia and the territory of Florida, (2) refuse to vote for government officials who would not act on these petitions, (3) protest the use of federal prisons for confining runaway slaves, (4) vote against any leaders who would allow new slave states to be admitted into the Union, (5) protest the injustice and cruelty of returning fugitive slaves to their owners without a jury trial, (6) cut their ties with slavery by selling their shares in Southern plantations and businesses, (7) stop supporting slavery by refusing to purchase goods produced by slave labor, and (8) strive to overcome racial prejudice. The Grimkés also suggested actions that Northern churches and ministers should take. Northern churches should prohibit slaveholders from participating in communion. Northern ministers should preach against slavery from their pulpits and should not remain silent concerning slavery when they had the opportunity to preach in southern churches.[104]

The second critical work directed at the Grimkés, the "Pastoral Letter," warned the sisters and other women like them who ventured outside their prescribed sphere of the dangers of such actions. In

---

[103]Juliana Tappan to Anne Weston, 21 July 1837 in Ceplair, *The Public Years of Sarah and Angelina Grimké*, 140.

[104]Sarah and Angelina Grimké to "Clarkson," 1 March 1837 in Barnes and Dumond, *Letters of Theodore Dwight Weld*, 1:369–71.

responding to this criticism of her work, Sarah relied on her personal conviction that she was obeying divine leadership. She believed God willed her involvement in the abolition movement and in the public defense of the right of women to work in the antislavery cause. Her correspondence of this time period reveals her determination to follow through on her commitment to fight slavery. To Henry Wright she wrote, "The Lord knows that we did not come to forward our own interest but in simple obedience to his commands and I do not believe we are responsible for the consequences of doing the will of God."[105]

Eventually, Sarah made a direct response to the criticism of her work by the Congregational ministers. Prior to the publication of the "Pastoral Letter," Sarah had been writing a series of letters that addressed the role of women. In the third letter of the series, that later was published as *Letters on the Equality of the Sexes* (1838), she answered the Congregational clergy's charges. To the clergy's demand that women return to their "appropriate duties and influence," Sarah wrote:

> The Lord Jesus defines the duties of his followers in his Sermon on the Mount. He lays down grand principles by which they should be governed, without reference to sex or condition.... I follow him through all his precepts, and find him giving the same directions to women as to men, never even referring the distinction now so strenuously insisted upon between masculine and feminine virtues: this is one of the anti-christian "traditions of men" which are taught instead of the "commandments of God." Men and women are CREATED EQUAL! They are both moral and accountable beings and whatever is *right* for man to do is *right* for woman.[106]

---

[105]Sarah Grimké to Henry C. Wright, 27 August 1837 in Barnes and Dumond, *Letters of Theodore Dwight Weld*, 1:437.

[106]Sarah Grimké, *Letters on the Equality of the Sexes and Other Essays*, ed. Elizabeth Ann Bartlett (New Haven: Yale University Press, 1988) 38.

"The Pastoral Letter," instead of persuading the sisters to discontinue their public work as abolitionists, prompted the Grimkés to work harder for the cause of abolition. The letter also led Sarah to articulate clearly and forcefully her views about women's rights. These rights included not only their right to work publicly as reformers but also their right to an education, to equal pay for equal work, and to a career.

Although still deeply committed to the antislavery cause, Sarah now knew that she could not separate the issues of abolition and women's rights. She felt compelled to speak not only about the abuses faced by slaves but also about the abuses encountered by women. As a result, she adamantly refused to remain silent on the issue of women's rights. Once again, she entered into a new area of social reform.

The reality that many of her fellow abolitionists, both male and female, also opposed her beliefs about women's rights disturbed Sarah. Despite such opposition, she stood firm in her commitment to her right as a woman to speak out against slavery. To Weld, who accused the Grimkés of neglecting the cause of abolition for the cause of women's rights, Sarah wrote: "We have kept steadily on with our A[nti-] S[lavery] work; we have not held one mtg. less.... Thou takes it for granted that our heads are so full of womans rights, womans rights that our hearts have grown cold in the cause of the slave, that we have started aside like broken bows. Now we think thou hast verily misjudged us."[107] Sarah continued by assuring him that abolition was still her main focus. Yet she also defended the right of all women to pray, to preach, and to speak against moral evils.

Sarah's dealings with abolitionists who questioned whether women had the right to speak publicly confirmed for her that what was at stake in this controversy was not just the right of women to

---

[107]Sarah Grimké to Theodore Weld, 20 September 1837, in Barnes and Dumond, *Letters of Theodore Dwight Weld*, 1:448.

have an equal role in the movement but the right of women to have an equal role in all areas of society. In her letter to Amos Phelps, one of the abolitionist leaders opposing women's rights, Sarah wrote and accused him of voicing the same oppressive views as the author of the "Pastoral Letter." She then proceeded to defend her own views on women's rights:

> We should regret that a brother whom we esteem so highly should identify himself with the man who sent forth the Pastoral Letter, a letter which aims to tear from woman her dearest rights and substitute the paltry privilege of leaning upon a fallen creature instead of the strong arm of Almighty God. We believe that this subject of womens rights and duties must come before the public for discussion, so that the Lord will help us to endure the opposition, contumely and scorn which will be cast upon womanhood and that he will make us more than conquerors thro' him that loved us. We would, therefore, entreat our brethren to stand still not for our sakes, but for their own, least [sic] peradventure they be found fighting against God.[108]

In this and other correspondence as well as in her lectures, Sarah defended her right to speak publicly.[109]

The Grimké sisters' inclusion of the theme of women's rights in their lectures and writings demonstrated their willingness to step outside the dominant culture of their day. Such presumptuousness irritated some ministers and abolitionists and infuriated others. Yet, within the abolition movement, there were both men and women

---

[108]Sarah M. Grimké to Amos A. Phelps, 3 August 1837, in Ceplair, *The Public Years of Sarah and Angelina Grimké*, 274–75.

[109]Lerner, *The Grimké Sisters From South Carolina*, 203. See also Blanche Glassman Hersh, "To Make the World Better: Protestant Women in the Abolitionist Movement," in *Triumph over Silence: Women in Protestant History*, ed. Richard L. Greaves (Westport CT: Greenwood Press, 1985) 183.

who endorsed the Grimkés' views on women's rights and encouraged the inclusion of such views in their speeches and publications.

Among the radical male abolitionists who supported Sarah and Angelina was William Lloyd Garrison. From the Grimkés' earliest days as abolitionists, they found Garrison to be a champion of women's rights.[110] He encouraged their participation in the movement and approved of their connecting the slavery issue with the women's rights issue. His approval of their work as abolitionists, however, proved to be beneficial to his own agenda. The ministerial attack on women's right to speak publicly set forth in the "Pastoral Letter" provided him with an excuse to declare all-out war on the clergy. In response to the attack, Garrison developed his doctrines of anti-institutional Christianity to their fullest.[111]

Perhaps the most faithful supporter of the Grimké sisters was Henry C. Wright. Early in their tour as abolitionist lecturers, Wright opened to them the doors of his home in Newburyport, Massachusetts, and by July 1837, they had begun to use his house as their headquarters. During the time the Grimkés' spent touring Massachusetts, Wright assisted them in scheduling their tour and in planning their lectures. He also acted as their escort during much of the tour.

In the summer of 1837, Wright sought to popularize the Grimkés' views on the woman question, and he published excerpts of their writings alongside his own in *The Liberator*. He titled the series "Labours of the Miss Grimkés."[112] His support proved to be

---

[110]Sarah Grimké to Henry C. Wright, 27 August 1837, in Barnes and Dumond, *Letters of Theodore Dwight Weld*, 1:438.

[111]Bass, "The Best Hopes of the Sexes,"162.

[112]*The Liberator*, 7 July, 21 July, 28 July, 4 August 1837. Wright's column and its endorsement of women's rights outraged many within the abolitionist movement. When Wright refused to discontinue writing the column, the New York Executive Committee of the Anti-Slavery Society transferred him to Philadelphia. See Lerner, *The Grimké Sisters From South Carolina*, 181–82.

essential to the reform work of Sarah and Angelina. Their persistence in the face of opposition may be attributed, in part, to his treatment of them as equals and to his encouragement of their continued intellectual development.[113] Both Sarah and Angelina recognized his significance to their work. In several of her letters during this period, Angelina praised Wright as "one of the best men I ever met with" and as "one of the holyest [*sic*] men I ever saw."[114]

Support for the Grimkés and their views on women's rights also came from women within the abolition movement, especially the women abolitionists of Boston. Maria Weston Chapman, a leader of the Boston Female Anti-Slavery Society, praised the contributions of Sarah and Angelina to the advancement of women. In her annual report to that society, Chapman applauded the Grimkés' efforts: "The example and teaching of the Grimkés wrought conviction as to the rights and consequent duties of women in the minds of multitudes.... Probably our children's children, our sons no less than our daughters, will dwell on the memory of these women, as the descendants of the bondman of today will cherish the name of Garrison."[115]

Chapman's sister and fellow leader in the society, Anne Warren Weston, also backed the work of the Grimkés. She made her support known in an open letter to the Boston Female Anti-Slavery Society: "The path that Sarah and Angelina Grimké have marked for themselves is one in which they will probably encounter much of

---

[113]Lerner, *The Grimké Sisters From South Carolina*, 178.

[114]Angelina Grimké to Jane Smith, 26 June 1837 and 25 July 1837, quoted in Ceplair, *The Public Years of Sarah and Angelina Grimké*, 140.

[115]Maria Weston Chapman, "Right and Wrong in Boston," *Annual Report of the Boston Female Anti-Slavery Society with a sketch of the obstacles thrown in the way of Emancipation by certain Clerical Abolitionists and Advocates for the subjection of woman in 1837* (Boston: Boston Female Anti-Slavery Society, 1837) 61. Quoted in Ceplair, *The Public Years of Sarah and Angelina Grimké*, 350.

suffering and persecution. As a Society we are determined as far as lies in our power to meet whatever awaits them."[116]

Other female abolitionists, including Mary Parker, president of the Boston Female Anti-Slavery Society, expressed their support for their Grimkés. In August 1837, following the Massachusetts clergymen's public criticism of Sarah and Angelina, Parker wrote the sisters and assured them that the Boston women would stand by them even if everyone else forsook them.[117] The encouragement received by the Grimkés from Garrison, Wright, and many of the abolitionist women to some extent eased the trials to which the sisters were subjected. Such support enabled the sisters to remain firm in their commitment to women's rights and to continue their tour of New England.

Early on during their speaking tour, Sarah and Angelina shared the podium as equals. Yet, as the weeks went by, Angelina began to gain greater recognition as a speaker, which may be attributed to her exceptional ability as a lecturer. Another factor in Angelina's rise in popularity was the fact that Sarah had begun to pull back from her opportunities to speak. Sarah suffered from bronchitis and colds during much of the tour. Yet poor health does not appear to have been the primary cause for her increasing reluctance to speak in public. The primary cause seems to have been the opposition she faced from male abolitionists. Her speeches, they contended, did not have the same quality as those of Angelina. As a result, male abolitionists, including Theodore Weld, encouraged Sarah to step back and allow Angelina to do all the speaking.[118]

Angelina, however, continued to encourage her sister to lecture. In her correspondence, Angelina often referred to Sarah as

---

[116]Anne Weston to Boston Female Anti-Slavery Society, 21 August 1837, Weston Papers, Boston Public Library, quoted in Ellen DuBois, "Struggling into Existence: The Feminism of Sarah and Angelina Grimké," *Women: A Journal of Liberation* 1/2 (Spring 1970): 6.

[117]Mary Parker to Angelina Grimké, 12 August 1837, in Barnes and Dumond, *Letters of Theodore Dwight Weld*, 1:419.

[118]Nies, *Seven Women*, 27.

the more gifted speaker.[119] Despite such encouragement, Sarah began to see her role as the supporter and encourager of her sister. For several months, Sarah carried her full share of lecturing and most likely the larger share of research and preparation. Even so, she began to discount her contributions to abolition. In a September 1837 letter to Sarah Douglass, Sarah wrote: "My precious sister has a gift in lecturing, in reasoning and elucidating, so far superior to mine that I know the cause is better pleaded if left entirely in her hands. My spirit has not bowed to this dispensation without prayer for resignation to being thus laid aside, but since I have been enabled to take the above view, I have been contented to be silent, believing that so is the will of God."[120] Despite Sarah's statement and despite the fact that she became the less visible and less outspoken of the sisters, she led the way in providing intellectual arguments against slavery and developing an approach to the "woman question."

On 3 November 1837, the abolition tour of Sarah and Angelina ended. It had lasted approximately six months. The sisters visited sixty-seven New England towns and addressed 40,500 people.[121] Both sisters now were exhausted, and Angelina had developed typhoid fever.[122] They spent the next few months resting and recovering from the strenuous activities of the past year. By early 1838, the Grimkés became involved once again in abolition work. They attended the annual meeting of the Massachusetts Anti-Slavery Society in January, lectured to antislavery meetings, and corresponded with abolitionist leaders, especially Weld.

In February 1838, Angelina became the first woman to address a legislative committee when she spoke before a committee of the Massachusetts House of Representatives. Her topic was the abolition of slavery, but she also spoke out in defense of women's

[119]Lerner, *The Grimké Sisters From South Carolina*, 172.

[120]Sarah Grimké to Sarah Douglass, September 1827, in Birney, *Sarah and Angelina Grimké*, 191.

[121]Hersh, *The Slavery of Sex*, 18.

[122]Lerner, *The Grimké Sisters From South Carolina*, 204.

right to participate in antislavery efforts.[123] Her speech profoundly impressed her audience and propelled her into the forefront as a leading female abolitionist of the period.

Angelina's public career as an abolitionist came to an end shortly after she addressed the legislative committee. Earlier in the year, her correspondence with Weld led to a romantic interest and eventually a marriage proposal. On 14 May 1838, Angelina and Weld were married in Philadelphia, and the next day, Angelina, along with Sarah, attended the Anti-Slavery Convention of American Women.[124] Angelina's speeches at the convention, despite her intentions and the intentions of her new husband, proved to be her last public antislavery effort for more than twenty-five years. Sarah's public abolition work also came to an end, although she did continue to write and promote the abolition cause. Thus, on 15 May 1838, after only nineteen months, Sarah's public career as an abolitionist came to an end. Her work as a reformer, however, was far from over.

---

[123]Melder, *Beginning of Sisterhood*, 91.
[124]Ceplair, *The Public Years of Sarah and Angelina Grimké*, 302.

Chapter 5

Feminism:
Sarah Grimké's Understanding
of Gender Equality

The first ardent and prominent American feminist was actually a man—the novelist Charles Brockden Brown. In 1796–1797, Brown produced the first American book devoted to the propagandizing of the rights of women, *Alcuin: A Dialogue of the Rights of Women*. The book, written in novel form, outlined a future utopia in which men and women lived as equals in every respect: economically, vocationally, and legally.[1] In this utopia, Brown argued that marriage would be based upon reason rather than emotion and that couples would be able to obtain divorces easily, thereby giving women some sense of equality in their most intimate relationships with men. The novel, despite the radicalness of its presentation, did not receive much attention due to its tedious writing style.

In 1818, Hannah Mather Crocker produced the next significant feminist writing in America, *Observations on the Real Rights of*

---

[1]Robert E. Riegel, *American Feminists* (Lawrence: University of Kansas Press, 1963) 7. See also Barbara J. Berg, *The Remembered Gate: Origins of American Feminism, The Woman and the City, 1800–1860* (New York: Oxford University Press, 1978) 18–19.

Women, with Their Appropriate Duties, Agreeable to Scripture, Reason and Common Sense. Despite its title, the book did not provide a clear articulation of feminist thought. Crocker, however, did argue that men and women had equal intellectual and moral capabilities, but she did not advocate that women be granted equality outside their traditional sphere—the home. Instead, Crocker merely encouraged her female readers to excel in their own sphere.[2]

The publication of the two previous books did not contribute as much to the early development of American feminism as did the work of a British author, Mary Wollstonecraft. In 1792, she published in England her pioneering work in feminist thought, *A Vindication of the Rights of Women.* The book was soon reprinted in the United States.[3] In her writings, Wollstonecraft attacked the traditional double standard of morals for men and women, the unequal decision-making process within marriage, and the lack of serious female education. Her candor about the sexual relationship of husbands and wives and her assertion that women experienced strong physical passions shocked most nineteenth-century Americans. Because of Wollstonecraft's personal disregard for the traditional standards of morality and her status as an unwed mother, most Americans disapproved of her work.[4]

Another Englishwoman whose work led to the advancement of feminist beliefs in America was Frances Wright. Unlike Wollstonecraft, Wright traveled to the United States in 1824 and spent much of the next six years lecturing in America on women's rights. She argued that the improvement of women's status would

---

[2]Riegel, *American Feminists,* 7–8.

[3]Mary Wollstonecraft, "A Vindication of the Rights of Women," in *The Feminist Papers: From Adams to de Beauvoir,* ed. Alice S. Rossi (New York: Columbia University Press, 1973) 40–85.

[4]Emily Hahn, *Once Upon a Pedestal* (New York: Thomas Y. Crowell Co., 1974) 28–30.

benefit men as well. Equality for women also would increase the civility, intelligence, and happiness of society as a whole.[5]

Wright set out to implement her feminist ideas by establishing a model community in Nashoba, near Memphis, Tennessee. Women there had complete freedom of action and complete equality in education, employment, and marriage. The American reaction to Wright was predictable given her radical views on the need for easily obtainable divorces, her stance on the appropriateness of the amalgamation of the races, and her own personal practice of sexual freedom and divorce. Americans labeled Wright "the Red Harlot of Infidelity" and "a female Tom Paine."[6] Even those persons open to feminism condemned her radical message.[7]

While all these individuals were influential in some spheres with regard to the introduction of feminism in America, their influence was limited and, more often than not, produced negative reactions. There were, however, several groups who elicited a more positive response and who had a more widespread impact. One of the groups that had a significant impact on the development of American feminism was the Quakers. Their doctrine of the "Inner Light," their belief in the spiritual equality of the sexes, and their acceptance of women holding positions of leadership within the church contributed to their influence on feminism. The enormity of the Society of Friends' impact is evident when one considers that many of the nineteenth-century American feminist leaders were Quakers: Lucretia Mott, Mary Ann McClintoch, Jane Hunt, and Martha Wright. Along with Elizabeth Cady Stanton, these four women met in 1848 at Seneca Falls, New York, to organize the first

---

[5]Elizabeth Ann Bartlett, Introduction to *Letters on the Equality of the Sexes and Other Essays, by Sarah Grimké* (New Haven: Yale University Press, 1988) 8–9.

[6]Riegel, *American Feminists*, 14.

[7]Blanche Glassman Hersh, *The Slavery of Sex: Feminist-Abolitionists in America* (Urbana: University of Illinois Press, 1978) 19.

women's rights convention. At least one-fourth of the women who signed that convention's Declaration of Sentiments were Quakers.[8]

A second American group that greatly influenced the development of feminism in the United States was the abolitionists. Although not all abolitionists endorsed equality for women, the most influential abolitionist, William Lloyd Garrison, advocated women's rights. Garrison was the "first major male leader to seek, secure, and sustain collective action to achieve" rights for women.[9] He argued that women had not only the right but the duty to work publicly to end the "degraded and insufferable condition" of members of their own sex.[10] Other abolitionists, including many women abolitionists, supported the feminist position and spoke out forcefully against the continued oppression of women.[11]

Because of the tendency of the Quakers and the abolitionist leaders to promote the rights of women, it is not surprising that Sarah and Angelina Grimké eventually adopted the feminist doctrine. Of the two Grimké sisters, Sarah became the more ardent feminist.[12] Angelina supported the feminist cause in her writings and speeches and did not hesitate to suggest that a parallel existed between the oppression of slaves and the oppression of women. Yet "the woman question" always remained a subordinate issue to abolition for Angelina.[13] For Sarah, however, the "woman question" took on primary importance. Her writings reflect her focus on the issue of feminism. In her first major writing, *Letters on the Equality of Sexes and the Condition of Women* (1838), she offered a

---

[8]Nancy A. Hewitt, "Feminist Friends: Agrarian Quakers and the Emergence of Woman's Rights in America," *Feminist Studies* 12/1 (Spring 1986): 29.

[9]Suzanne M. Marilley, *Woman Suffrage and the Origins of Liberal Feminism in the United States, 1820–1920* (Cambridge: Harvard University Press, 1996) 16.

[10]*The Liberator*, 7 January 1832.

[11]Hersh, *Slavery of Sex*, 20–22.

[12]Bartlett, Introduction to *Letters on the Equality of the Sexes*, 1.

[13]Ibid.

controversial yet innovative affirmation of the rights of women.[14] Her convictions about the need for full female equality are reflected in what has become the most often quoted passage of her writings: "I ask no favors for my sex. I surrender not our claim to equality. All I ask of our brethren is, that they will take their feet from our necks, and permit us to stand upright on that ground which God designed us to occupy."[15]

---

[14]The letters contained in *Letters on the Equality of the Sexes and the Condition of Women* first appeared in 1837 in the *New England Spectator*. Sarah began writing the letters for this newspaper early in July. The fifteen letters were titled: "The Original Equality of Woman," "Woman Subject Only to God," "The Pastoral Letter of the General Association of Congregational Ministers of Massachusetts," "Social Intercourse of the Sexes," "Condition in Asia and Africa," "Women in Asia and Africa," "Condition in Some Parts of Europe and America," "On the Condition of Women in the United States," "Heroism of Women—Women in Authority," "Intellect of Woman," "Dress of Women," "Legal Disabilities of Women," "Relation of Husband and Wife," "Ministry of Women," and "Man Equally Guilty with Woman in the Fall." In 1838, the letters were collected and published in Boston by Isaac Knapp Publishers. Subsequent citations from these letters are from Elizabeth Bartlett's collection of Sarah's writings and do not include references to particular letters.

Although Sarah's letters dealing with women in Europe, Asia, and Africa are not addressed in this book, the content of these letters is interesting. Sarah chronicled the condition of women in each of these geographic regions, analyzed the laws that affected them, addressed the injuries suffered by them, and examined the educational and vocational opportunities available to them. She summed up the treatment received by women in Asia and Africa by stating that they had either been made slaves by men or had been dressed like dolls and used as toys to amuse men. European women, Sarah said, had not been as uniformly or as deeply debased as women in other parts of the world. Yet, even in Europe, a woman did not have the opportunity to fulfill "the high station she was designed to occupy as a moral and intellectual being." See Sarah M. Grimké, *Letters on the Equality of the Sexes and Other Essays*, ed. Elizabeth Ann Bartlett (New Haven: Yale University Press, 1988) 51.

[15]Grimké, *Letters on the Equality of the Sexes*, 35.

Sarah's production of these letters was, in part, a response to criticism directed toward her and Angelina by Congregational ministers belonging to the General Association of Massachusetts. On 28 July 1837, these ministers endorsed a document titled "Pastoral Letter of the General Association of Massachusetts to the Congregational Churches under their care." The "Pastoral Letter" cited biblical evidence that supported their denouncement of women who assumed "the place and tone of man as a public reformer."[16] The letter also claimed that God ordained women's dependence upon men and that women who usurped the authority of men violated God's command. Although the letter did not mention the Grimkés by name, the authors of the letter clearly were targeting Sarah and Angelina and were criticizing the sisters' emphasis on the right of women to work publicly for the abolition of slavery.

At the time the "Pastoral Letter" circulated, Angelina was in constant demand as a speaker, and her lectures occupied most of her time. Thus, the task of providing a public defense of women's rights against the attack of the Congregational ministers fell to Sarah. Beginning in July 1837, when she was forty-four years old, Sarah began writing a series for the *New England Spectator* titled "Letters on the Province of Women." She used one of these letters to respond to the criticisms directed at her and her sister by the Congregational ministers. This and the other letters were published in 1838 as *Letters on the Equality of the Sexes, and the Condition of Woman*, which proved to be the first serious discussion of women's rights by an American woman.[17] Anne Firor Scott says of Sarah's *Letters on the Equality of the Sexes*: "These letters constitute a lucid

---

[16]"Pastoral Letter: The General Association of Massachusetts to the Churches Under Their Care," *The Public Years of Sarah and Angelina Grimké: Selected Writings, 1835–1839*, ed. Larry Ceplair (New York: Columbia University Press, 1989) 211.

[17]Blanche Glassman Hersh, "To Make the World Better: Protestant Women in the Abolitionist Movement," in *Triumph over Silence: Women in Protestant History*, ed. Richard L. Greaves (Westport CT: Greenwood Press, 1985) 183.

critique of the whole nineteenth-century image of woman, and of the effect it had upon the lives of women—particularly upon women's education, upon what women were led by custom to expect and upon their legal status, and upon women's own choices of the way they spent that most precious commodity, time."[18] In refuting the arguments of those who condemned women's rights to educational, vocational, personal, and spiritual equality and to support her views on the equality of women, Sarah appealed to insight from Enlightenment thought, the notion of human perfectibility, and the Bible.

Sarah had not been trained in Enlightenment thinking, nor did she possess "a broad grounding in philosophy." Yet she attempted to make up for her educational deficiencies through studying and reading.[19] In the course of her personal studies, she read writings by John Locke and Thomas Jefferson, and as she wrote *Letters on the Equality of the Sexes*, Sarah began to incorporate some of the vocabulary and principles she found in Locke, Jefferson, and other Enlightenment writers.[20] These Enlightenment thinkers scrutinized religious, historical, linguistic, political, and social structures, and as a result, the Enlightenment ushered in an era of critical inquiry, an era in which persons reevaluated the hierarchical constructs of their culture.[21] In her writings, Sarah implemented several of the Enlightenment themes such as liberty, equality, natural rights, and education. Indeed, many of the nineteenth-century feminist arguments relied on Enlightenment presuppositions that emphasized

---

[18]Anne Firor Scott, *The Southern Lady: From Pedestal to Politics, 1830–1930* (Chicago: University of Chicago Press, 1970) 61–62.

[19]Elizabeth Bartlett, *Liberty, Equality, Sorority: The Origins and Interpretation of American Feminist Thought: Francis Wright, Sarah Grimké, and Margaret Fuller* (Brooklyn NY: Carlson Publishing, 1994) 62.

[20]Gerda Lerner, *The Feminist Thought of Sarah Grimké* (New York/Oxford: Oxford University Press, 1998) 21.

[21]Peter Gay, *The Enlightenment: An Interpretation, the Rise of Modern Paganism* (New York: W. W. Norton and Co., 1966) 150.

the orderliness and rationality of the universe and that maintained that universal truths could be discovered through reason and observation.

One idea held by Enlightenment philosophers concerned the proper understanding of "human nature." They concluded that the human mind was a "blank slate" at birth and that educational and environmental experiences shaped human nature. Such a view of human nature had significant implications for the feminist argument, and early feminists such as Wright and Wollstonecraft relied on these Enlightenment ideas in their defense of the need for equal educational and social opportunities for women.[22]

Sarah was also influenced by such Enlightenment thinking. Like Wollstonecraft and Wright, she denounced the inferior opportunities women encountered in every sphere of life and argued that women should have equal educational, economic, and vocational rights and opportunities. Like other feminists, Sarah emphasized education and the law as means by which women could gain freedom and equality. The need of women to gain such freedom and equality was self-evident and "need only to be examined to be understood and asserted."[23] Sarah, however, did not accept the Enlightenment idea of "blank slates." She believed that humans entered the world as souls, and as beings with souls, men and women both were created to be moral and responsible agents. Committed to the doctrine of original sin, Sarah concluded that the sin of Adam and Eve tainted all men and women. Because all humans shared in the guilt of Adam and Eve, they could not be considered as innocent and therefore were not "blank slates."[24]

One outgrowth of Enlightenment doctrines was "liberalism," a political philosophy articulated by natural law theorists such as John Locke and Thomas Jefferson and then by utilitarians such as Jeremy Bentham and John Stuart Mill.[25] Natural law theorists sought to

---

[22]Bartlett, Introduction to *Letters on the Equality of the Sexes*, 6–7.

[23]Grimké, *Letters on The Equality of the Sexes*, 38.

[24]Bartlett, *Liberty, Equality, Sorority*, 66.

[25]Gay, *The Enlightenment*, 18.

guarantee the natural rights to life, liberty, and property to all men. Jefferson's "Declaration of Independence" echoed these themes of classical natural law theory. Feminists, including Sarah, sought to extend these rights to women as well as to men. As a nineteenth-century American, she committed herself to the ideal that the nation had been founded on the principles of equality and freedom. Yet she recognized that only through reform efforts such as abolitionism and the fight for women's rights could America embody its ideals. Slaves and women both must be freed in order for her country to live up to its high calling.[26]

The liberal political tradition continued to emphasize liberty, but as a result of the influence of Bentham and of Mill, it moved away from the standard of natural rights to the principle of utilitarianism. The utilitarian maxim for good government is summed up as "the greatest good for the greatest number."[27] Sarah relied on this standard in her attempt to justify female equality. She argued that men and society in general, not just women, would benefit from women being given greater freedom. It was destructive both to women and *men*, she said, for women to be treated as parasites. She further argued that if women felt the responsibility to support themselves, it would add "strength and dignity to their characters, and teach them more true sympathy for their husbands...a sympathy which would be exhibited by actions as well as words."[28] An improvement in women's status, Sarah reasoned, would ensure the well-being of society.[29]

---

[26]Carolyn De Swarte Gifford, "American Women and the Bible: The Nature of Woman as a Hermeneutical Issue," in *Feminist Perspectives on Biblical Scholarship*, ed. Adela Yarbro Collins (Chico CA.: Scholars Press, 1985) 18 and Rosemary Radford Ruether, "The Subordination and Liberation of Women in Christian Theology: St. Paul and Sarah Grimké," *Soundings* 61/2 (Summer 1978): 177.

[27]Bartlett, *Liberty, Equality, Sorority*, 14.

[28]Grimké, *Letters on the Equality of the Sexes*, 61.

[29]Ibid., 57–58, 61.

Clearly Sarah advocated much of the rhetoric of rights that emerged during the Enlightenment, and she borrowed both ideas and terminology from Enlightenment thinkers.[30] Yet like most feminists of her day, she did not state such Enlightenment ideas in a formal or systematic way. The lack of a systematic presentation is understandable given the fact that Sarah was not a philosopher but was primarily an activist and propagandist.[31]

Sarah's development of feminism also was influenced by her understanding of the concept of human perfectibility. In the nineteenth century, those holding to the ideals of perfectionism believed that if people obeyed the dictates of their consciences, they would achieve perfect holiness. Many of the abolitionists in Boston in the 1830s held to such ideals. The adherence of these Boston abolitionists to perfectionism led many of them to endorse the feminist idea that "men and women not only *could* but should, *change*—and in the direction of minimizing sex differences."[32] When the Grimké sisters arrived in Boston in May 1837, Henry Wright, Lydia Child, and Maria Chapman warmly welcomed Sarah and Angelina and willing shared perfectionist ideals with them.

Dorothy Bass suggests three elements central to the Boston abolitionists' perfectionism and their subsequent adoption of gender equality. First, the perfectionists rejected "outward forms" as irrelevant. Thus, rituals of worship such as baptism had no bearing on their understanding of true worship, nor did sexually-

---

[30]Bartlett cautions that the argument that Sarah relied on the Enlightenment ideology of human rights in her defense of feminism should not be accepted without distinguishing between the idea of having rights and the governing rules or moral principles that define the substance of those rights. She writes, "Certainly the rhetoric of rights emerged from the Enlightenment, and Grimké borrowed the idea and terminology, but it is not clear that the rules on which Grimké's concept of rights is based comes from the Enlightenment. The source of Grimké's concept of rights is found not in the term rights, but in the governing rules and principles." See Bartlett, *Liberty, Equality, Sorority*, 65.

[31]Hersh, The Slavery of Sex, 191.

[32]Ibid., 206.

differentiated bodies contain any clue as to the moral nature of the souls they represented.[33] In her *Letters on the Equality of the Sexes*, Sarah adopted this ideal and firmly rejected any notion that gender was significant to moral accountability. She asserted: "Men and women were CREATED EQUAL; they are both moral and accountable being."[34]

Second, these perfectionists espoused anti-denominationalism and anti-clericalism. Most had been disillusioned by the churches' apathy toward the cause of slavery and had left behind organized religion. Their anti-clerical views now allowed them to argue that women no longer had to have clerical approval to participate in reform efforts.[35] Sarah could appreciate such sentiments following her disastrous relationship with the Society of Friends and the circulation of the "Pastoral Letter." She came to believe that no government, either civil or ecclesiastical, deserved obedience. In a letter to Gerrit Smith, Sarah wrote: "The more I contemplate this sublime doctrine of acknowledgeing [*sic*] no government but Gods [*sic*], of losing myself from all dominion of man both civil and ecclesiastical, the more I am persuaded it is the only doctrine that can bring us into that liberty wherewith Christ hath made us free."[36] Sarah also expressed a growing contempt for institutional religion in *Letters on the Equality of the Sexes*: "It is manifest, that if women were permitted to be ministers of the gospel, as they unquestionably were in the primitive ages of the Christian church, it would interfere materially with the present organized system of spiritual power and

---

[33]Dorothy C. Bass, "'The Best Hopes of the Sexes': The Woman Question in Garrisonian Abolitionism" (Ph.D. diss., Brown University, 1980) 163–64.

[34]Grimké, *Letters on the Equality of the Sexes*, 38.

[35]Bass, "The Best Hopes of the Sexes,"163–64.

[36]Sarah Grimké to Gerrit Smith, 28 June 1837, in Gilbert H. Barnes and Dwight L. Dumond, ed. *Letters of Theodore Dwight Weld, Angelina Grimké Weld, and Sarah Grimké, 1822–1844* (New York: Da Capo Press, 1970) 1:408.

ecclesiastical authority, which is now vested solely in the hands of men."[37]

Finally, the Boston abolitionists embraced the idea that all of life, not just one's private life, must be made holy and perfect. Their involvement in abolition and their defense of women's rights was demonstrative of their willingness to work in eradicating social evils.[38] Sarah's speeches and her writings clearly reflect that she too understood her role as a reformer of all of life—both public and private.

The abolitionists of Boston also introduced Sarah to the teachings and writings of John Humphrey Noyes.[39] Noyes, author of *The Perfectionist,* wrote that Christians could live in sinless perfection and that the way to the perfection lay through union with Christ. He believed that socialism was the means by which perfected Christians could bring the kingdom of heaven to earth. To demonstrate how his ideas could be lived out, Noyes, in 1840, established the Oneida community in Putney, Vermont.[40] These perfectionist ideals of Noyes and of the Boston abolitionists later surfaced in the writings of Sarah.

While Sarah incorporated the terminology and the ideas of the Enlightenment writers and while she adopted some of the teachings of perfectionism, the greatest source of Sarah's feminism was the Bible. Sarah relied heavily on her interpretation of scripture as she sought to defend the full equality of women. She began her discourse on woman's equality, *Letters on the Equality of Women*, by declaring that she would demonstrate the scriptural basis of female equality.

By employing the Bible to support her arguments, Sarah recognized that she would challenge the traditional and accepted interpretation of biblical texts. In her response to the "Pastoral

---

[37]Grimké, *Letters on the Equality of the Sexes*, 98.

[38]Bass, "The Best Hopes of the Sexes," 164.

[39]Bartlett, *Liberty, Equality, Sorority*, 64.

[40]Mark Noll, *A History of Christianity in the United States and Canada* (Grand Rapids: William B. Eerdmans Publishing Company, 1992) 197.

Letter," Sarah set forth her resolution to break away from what she perceived to be faulty biblical interpretation:

> In attempting to comply with thy request to give my views on the Province of Woman, I feel that I am venturing on nearly untrodden ground, and that I shall advance arguments in opposition to a corrupt public opinion, and to the perverted interpretation of Holy Writ, which has so universally obtained. But I am in search of truth; and no obstacle shall prevent my prosecuting the search…. In examining this important subject I shall depend solely on the Bible to designate the sphere of woman, because I believe that almost every thing that has been written on this subject, has been the result of a misconception of the simple truths revealed in the Scripture, in consequence of the false translation of many passages of Holy Writ.[41]

Because many biblical texts seemed to support the concept and the practice of the subordination of women, Sarah understood that she would have to offer a new interpretation of scripture, that is, a new hermeneutic.

Sarah was not, however, the first woman to develop a scriptural argument to defend the rights of women. In 1667, Margaret Fell, wife of George Fox, wrote a pamphlet titled *Women's Speaking Justified*. Fell produced this pamphlet while serving a prison sentence for holding Quaker beliefs. Despite Sarah's Quaker background, she was not familiar with Fell's writings or with this pamphlet, which was printed only one time and was not reprinted in the United States until the twentieth century.[42] Other feminists also had offered biblical interpretations prior to the time Sarah wrote *Letters on the Equality of the Sexes*, but she was unaware of these works. Thus, although Sarah was not the first to articulate a feminist

---

[41]Grimké, *Letters on the Equality of the Sexes*, 31.
[42]Lerner, *The Feminist Thought of Sarah Grimké*, 21.

understanding of scripture, her unfamiliarity with these other writers means that her biblical interpretations are wholly original and uniquely her own.[43]

In her defense of the equality of women, Sarah set forth the idea that God did not intend to subordinate women to men. She instead contended that male translators and interpreters of the Bible had introduced and propagated the mistaken concept of subordination. These translators and interpreters then continued to uphold subordination because it reflected their particular cultures and supported their own opinions regarding normative relationships between males and females. Unfortunately for women, subordination became the basis for defining womanhood and for establishing a woman's appropriate sphere of influence.[44]

Because she had serious doubts about men's ability to provide unbiased translations and interpretations of scripture, Sarah exhorted women to produce a new hermeneutic.[45] She believed that once women had the scholarly tools necessary for the study of scripture, they could construct an accurate interpretation.[46] Sarah declared that women "must enter [their] protest against the false translation of some passages by the MEN who did that work, and against the perverted interpretation by the MEN who undertook to write commentaries thereon. I am inclined to think, when we are admitted to the honor of studying Greek and Hebrew, we shall produce some various readings of the Bible a little different from those we have now."[47] This claim to have the right to interpret scripture for oneself was a product of the influence of Protestantism. Sarah was acquainted with the concept of "priesthood of believer" that originated with Martin Luther in his sixteenth-century fight against the Catholic Church, and in her conclusion to the first letter

---

[43]Ibid., 22.

[44]Gifford, "American Women and the Bible," 19.

[45]Marie Anne Mayeski, *Women: Models of Liberation* (Kansas City MO: Sheed and Ward, 1988) 161.

[46]Grimké, *Letters on the Equality of the Sexes*, 38.

[47]Ibid.

in *Letters on the Equality of the Sexes*, Sarah adapted Luther's famous statement at the Diet of Worms in 1521 and stated, "Here then I plant myself. God created us equal."[48] Thus, Sarah informed her audience of her intent to read and interpret the Bible without the assistance of clergymen, and she also notified her readers that she intended to correct the mistaken concept of subordination even though it meant denouncing the teachings of men such as those who composed the "Pastoral Letter."

Sarah began to implement her convictions about interpreting biblical passages for herself. She began by offering a new reading of the Old Testament. In the nineteenth century, American society accepted the prevalent interpretation of the Old Testament that supported a hierarchical structure in male-female relationships, with men being superior to women. Sarah attributed the popularizing of such an interpretation to John Milton, author of *Paradise Lost*. In his book, Milton offered a fictitious account of creation and the fall, which included a conversation between Adam and Eve. During this conversation, Eve acknowledged her inferiority to her husband. Milton has Eve say to Adam:

> My author and disposer, what thou bidst,
> Unargued I obey; so God ordains—
> God is thy law, thou mine: to know no more,
> Is woman's happiest knowledge and her praise.[49]

Sarah rejected Milton's account and interpretation of the Garden experience, and she especially deplored his portrait of Eve: "His Eve is embellished with every personal grace, to gratify the eye

---

[48]Grimké, *Letters on the Equality of the Sexes*, 34. These closing words in Sarah's first letter echo the words of Martin Luther in 1521: "Here I stand. I can do no other." See James M. Kittelson, *Luther the Reformer: The Story of the Man and His Career* (Minneapolis: Augsburg Publishing House, 1986) 161.

[49]John Milton, *Paradise Lost*, quoted in Grimké, *Letters on the Equality of the Sexes*, 81.

of her admiring husband; but he seems to have furnished the mother of mankind with just intelligence enough to comprehend her supposed inferiority to Adam, and to yield unresisting submission to her lord and master."[50] Such a portrait of Eve, and of women in general, was "fraught with absurdity and wickedness."[51] Sarah concluded that if it were a true portrait, the first commandment of the Decalogue would have to be rewritten as: "Man shall have no other gods before ME, and woman shall have no other gods before MAN."[52] Instead of accepting that Hebrew scriptures support male dominance, Sarah reinterpreted them in such a way as to show that, from the beginning of history, God intended the equality of men and woman.

Sarah argued that the creation accounts in Genesis 1–2 and the account of the fall in Genesis 3 provided two foundational principles: God created both man and woman in the image of God, and God gave man and woman dominion over all other creatures but not over one another. The first principle, according to Sarah, was supported by the creation stories. In her examination of these stories, Sarah began with Genesis 1:27, which reads, "So God created man in his own image, in the image of God created he him, male and female created he them."[53] Of this account of creation, she wrote: "In all this sublime description of the creation of man, (which is a generic term including man and woman), there is not one particle of difference intimated as existing between them. They were both made in the image of God."[54]

Because God created both man and woman in the divine image, Sarah argued that they were created in perfect equality.[55] The

---

[50]Ibid.

[51]Ibid.

[52]Ibid.

[53]All scripture passages are quoted from the King James Version, which was the version used by Sarah in her study of biblical passages dealing with women.

[54]Grimké, *Letters on the Equality of the Sexes*, 32.

[55]Ibid.

second account of creation in Genesis 2 provided Sarah with another means of justifying the equality of the sexes. According to that narrative, God created woman to be man's companion. The only way in which a woman could be a true companion to a man, Sarah contended, was to be his equal. She explained:

> It was not, therefore, merely to give man a creature susceptible of loving, obeying, and looking up to him, for all that the animals could do and did do. It was to give him a companion, *in all respects* his equal; one who was like himself *a free agent*, gifted with intellect and endowed with immortality; not a partaker merely of his animal gratifications, but able to enter into all his feelings as a moral and responsible being.[56]

Thus, for Sarah, a woman could not fulfill her divinely ordained role as a man's companion unless treated as an equal.

Even though the creation accounts provided the basis for Sarah's development of an Old Testament defense of female equality, she could not neglect the more difficult passages. The last part of Genesis 3:16, which records God saying to Eve, "Thy desire shall be to thy husband, and he shall rule over thee," was one of the passages of the Old Testament most often cited to support the subordination of woman to man. In her study of this passage, Sarah turned to the commentaries of Matthew Henry, a Welsh biblical commentator and a Presbyterian minister during the late seventeenth century and early eighteenth century. Henry, in commenting on Genesis 3:16, argued that the initial design of creation included the subordination of women to men. Subjection and obedience, therefore, were a woman's duties from the beginning of history. Such duties, according to Henry, became punishments only after Eve sinned against God. Henry contended that Eve's complaints concerning her subordinate position may be attributed to her fallen

---

[56]Ibid. Emphasis is Sarah's.

nature. Before sin entered the world, Eve seemed content in her role as Adam's inferior. After the fall, however, she despised her subjection to him. Henry concluded his exposition on Genesis 3:16 by stating that any woman who disobeyed her husband and who despised her subordinate position violated divine law and usurped God's original design for male-female relationships.[57]

Sarah, however, rejected Henry's interpretation as well as the traditional translation of Genesis 3:16. She pointed out that by changing the verb form from "shall" to "will" the passage could be read as God's prediction of women's lot in a fallen creation rather than as God's timeless commandment for women.[58] She wrote:

> The truth is that the curse, as it is termed, which was pronounced by Jehovah upon woman, is a simple prophecy. The Hebrew, like our French language, uses the same word to express shall and will. Our translators having been accustomed to exercise lordship over their wives, and seeing only through the medium of perverted judgement [sic], very naturally, though I think not very learnedly or very kindly, translated it shall instead of will, and thus converted a prediction to Eve into a command to Adam.[59]

Sarah also observed that the story of Cain and Abel (Gen. 5:2-15) used this same type of language. That text, she said, "was a prophecy of the dominion which Cain would usurp over his brother, and which issued in the murder of Abel."[60] Thus, Sarah concluded that man's superiority over woman portrayed in Genesis 3:16 was descriptive not prescriptive. In other words, instead of stating that man's superiority is the way things ought to be; it describes the way

---

[57]Matthew Henry, *Commentary on the Whole Bible*, ed. Leslie F. Church (Grand Rapids: Zondervan Publishing House, 1961) 11.

[58]Grimké, *Letters on the Equality of the Sexes*, 33.

[59]Ibid., 33.

[60]Ibid., 78.

things are as a result of sin and, therefore, a perversion of the way things ought to be.

The second Old Testament principle Sarah used centered upon her understanding that man and woman had dominion over other animals, not over one another. She argued that the idea that women were created inferior to men and destined to remain inferior contradicted the will of God. In assigning man the task of having dominion over the earth and the creatures of the earth, God never classified woman as one of those creatures over which man had dominion.[61] Instead, Sarah stated that "Jehovah could not surrender his authority to govern his own immortal creatures into the hands of a being, whom he knew, and whom his whole history proved, to be unworthy of a trust so sacred and important."[62] Even after the fall, when Adam and Eve "had incurred the penalty of sin, they were shorn of their innocence, but they stood on the same platform side by side, acknowledging *no superior* but their God."[63]

The fall, however, did have repercussions for the status of women. Sarah attributed man's lust for dominion over woman to the fallen state of humanity. Yet she argued that even in their fallenness, God had not subordinated women to the commands and desires of men. To support her argument, Sarah pointed to the Decalogue (Exod 20), which contains no instructions about women obeying their husbands. The first commandment of the Decalogue commands both women and their husbands to have no God but Jehovah and to bow down and serve no one other than God.[64]

Based on her interpretation of these Old Testament passages, Sarah concluded that in God's original plan of creation, men and women were created equal, endowed with the same human nature. Male domination, however, had violated that original plan, and thus for Sarah, "the appearance of women's inferiority in intellect or leadership ability is the product of distorted socialization, not of

---

[61]Ibid., 32.
[62]Ibid., 35.
[63]Ibid., 34. Emphasis is Sarah's.
[64]Ibid., 80.

nature."[65] This conclusion led Sarah to call her readers to overturn centuries of oppression against women and to challenge them to return to the true teaching about womanhood found in what she considered to be the original Old Testament message of freedom and equality.[66]

Not only did Sarah claim that the Old Testament had been misinterpreted and mistranslated; she also argued that the New Testament had been subjected repeatedly to faulty interpretations and translations. Believing that the themes of equality and liberation dominated the New Testament, especially in the teachings of Jesus, she judged the institutionalized relationships between men and women by these themes.

In her study of the New Testament, Sarah came to believe that Jesus championed the equality and freedom of women. She found that in the Sermon on the Mount, in which Jesus addressed both men and women, he made no reference to any distinctions between the sexes. Instead, he instituted principles by which the sexes should be governed. Sarah wrote of Jesus' words in the Sermon on the Mount:

> I follow him through all his precepts, and find him giving the same directions to women as to men, never even referring to the distinction now so strenuously insisted upon between masculine and feminine virtues: this is one of the anti-christian "traditions of men" which are taught instead of the "commandments of God." Men and women were CREATED EQUAL: they are both moral and accountable

---

[65]Rosemary Ruether, "Christianity," in *Women in World Religions*, ed. by Arvind Sharma (Albany: State University of New York Press, 1987) 230.

[66]Gifford, "American Women and the Bible," 19. See also Frank G. Kirkpatrick, "From Shackles to Liberation: Religion, the Grimké Sisters and Dissent," in *Women, Religion, and Social Change*, ed. Yvonne Yazbeck and Ellison Banks Findly (Albany: State University of New York Press, 1985) 444.

beings, and whatever is right for man to do, is right for woman.[67]

Sarah also noted that Jesus failed to offer a command for wives to obey their husbands. She reasoned that this omission in a sermon replete with the practical precepts of religion must have been intentional, and she concluded that the omission was proof that Jesus regarded men and women as equals.[68] Sarah recognized that appealing to Jesus' example would not settle the issue concerning women's equality. Proponents of male superiority often ignored the teachings of Jesus and instead relied on citations from Paul's epistles to defend their position. Thus, Sarah knew that she needed to deal with Paul's writings.

Before attempting to discern the meaning of Paul's writings, Sarah established two premises. Her first premise was that past explanations of his writings did not have to be accepted simply because these explanations had been venerated for generations. Sarah, therefore, challenged the notion that biblical interpretations could not be subjected to reexamination. She claimed the freedom, right, and responsibility to think for herself. Sarah wrote: "I was educated to think for myself, and it is a privilege I shall always claim to exercise."[69] Her second premise was that Paul had been influenced by Jewish prejudices. Sarah pointed to Paul's willingness to take a Nazirite vow, to offer sacrifices, and to circumcise Timothy as evidence of this influence. While Sarah believed Paul's writings to be inspired by God, she also noted that they must be read with the understanding of his own biases.[70] She concluded: "I do not conceive that I derogate in the least from his character as an inspired apostle, to suppose that he may have been imbued with the prevalent prejudices against women."[71]

---

[67]Grimké, *Letters on the Equality of the Sexes*, 38.
[68]Ibid., 80.
[69]Ibid., 81.
[70]Ibid.
[71]Ibid.

After examining Paul's writings, Sarah focused her attention on
a subject that was and continues to be a source of controversy:
Paul's command that women remain silent in the church. Paul
clearly stated this command in 1 Corinthians 14:34: "Let your
women keep silence in the churches, for it is not permitted unto
them to speak." Sarah recognized that she would need to reevaluate
the traditional understanding of this command and provide a new
interpretation of Paul's words. After much study, she surmised that
Paul's intention was not to prevent women from public speaking.
Instead, Paul's instructions were designed to correct the abuses of
both men and women in the Corinthian church.[72] Proof of her
assertion, Sarah argued, was that in the same letter Paul commanded
some of the men in the congregation to be silent (1 Cor 14:28).
Apparently, the Corinthian church struggled with the disorderly
conduct during worship services.[73] Sarah believed that Paul's words
in 1 Corinthians 14 were:

> Evidently designed to correct abuses which had crept
> into the assemblies of Christians in Corinth. Hence we find
> that the men were commanded to be silent, as well as the
> women, when they were guilty of any thing which deserved
> reprehension.... The men were doubtless in the practice of
> speaking in unknown tongues, when there was no interpreter
> present; and Paul reproves them, because this kind of
> preaching conveyed no instruction to the people.[74]

Thus, Sarah concluded that this verse cannot be used to justify
the silencing women in church.

Sarah also reinterpreted 1 Timothy 2:11–12, a second passage
in which Paul called for women to learn in silence. In those verses,
Paul commanded, "Let the woman learn in silence with all
subjection. But I suffer not a woman to teach, nor to usurp authority

---

[72]Ibid., 93.
[73]Ibid.
[74]Ibid.

over the man, but to be in silence." Sarah believed that instead of referring to public ministry by women, Paul was seeking to teach Timothy about proper conduct in worship. Once again, Sarah concluded that Paul's instructions were directed to female disciples who apparently interrupted worship services by asking questions. She wrote, "It is highly probable that women who had long been in bondage, when set free by Christianity from restraints imposed upon them by Jewish traditions and heathen customs, run into an extreme in their public assemblies, and interrupted the religious services by frequent interrogations, which they could have had answered as satisfactorily at home."[75]

According to Sarah, translators and commentators refused to recognize the historical context of these verses, which caused the continued misunderstanding of Paul's intentions concerning women speaking in public worship services.[76] Sarah also chastised those men and women who continually pointed to 1 Corinthians 14:34 to prove that women should not be allowed to speak publicly in church and yet condoned the participation of women as Sunday school teachers and choir members. She reminded these men and women of the need to be consistent in interpreting the scripture.[77]

A second issue raised by Paul's writings about women concerned his understanding of the public roles that women could hold in the church. The traditional interpretation of Paul's teachings on this subject was that the apostle saw no place for women as leaders in the church. Sarah, however, concluded that the apostle had not condemned female leadership roles in the church. The fact that Philip's daughters (Acts 21:8–9), Priscilla (Acts 18, Rom 16:3, 1 Cor 16:19), and Phoebe (Rom 16:1) served as prophetesses, teachers, and ministers in the early church and that Paul appeared to be aware of their work substantiated the appropriateness of women holding positions of leadership.[78]

---

[75]Ibid., 95.
[76]Ibid.
[77]Ibid., 97.
[78]Ibid., 91, 97–98.

Sarah also dealt with the passage most often cited by those persons who argued against women ministers holding leadership positions in the church: 1 Timothy 2. Sarah began by pointing out that the original text of the scriptures lacked punctuation and verse and chapter divisions and that the later addition of punctuation and of verse and chapter divisions often distorted the intent of the writers and the flow of the texts.[79] Sarah argued that 1 Timothy 2, especially verses 8 and 9, provided one example of the problematic nature of the insertion of verse and chapter divisions. In those verses, Paul wrote of the duty of prayer and of the need for women to adorn themselves in modest apparel: "I will therefore that men pray every where, lifting up holy hands, without wrath and doubting. In like manner also, that women adorn themselves in modest apparel, with shamefacedness and sobriety; not with broided [sic] hair, or gold, or pearls, or costly array." Sarah interpreted these verses based on her reading of the work of Joseph John Gurney, an early nineteenth-century English Bible Scholar and Quaker philanthropist. Gurney offered the following comments on this passage: "It is worded in a manner somewhat obscure; but appears to be best construed according to the opinion of various commentators as conveying an injunction, that women as well as men should pray everywhere, lifting holy hands without wrath and doubting."[80]

Sarah agreed with Gurney's interpretation and argued further that the translators would never have altered the passage had it not been for their own prejudices against women holding public positions of leadership. The references to apparel, Sarah claimed, were instructions for female ministers. Thus, Paul's words demonstrated his concern about the need for women leaders in the church to dress appropriately and not to call attention to themselves

---

[79]Ibid., 94.

[80]Joseph John Gurney, quoted in Grimké, *Letters on the Equality of the Sexes*, 94.

by wearing elaborate clothing or jewelry when performing their ministerial functions.[81]

Those persons who argued against women ministers also cited 1 Timothy 2:12 to support their argument. In that verse, Paul stated that he did not permit women to teach or have authority over men. The word "teach" was how most male commentators translated the Greek word *authentein* in that verse, but Sarah argued that a better translation of this word would be "dictate." Thus, according to Sarah, Paul intended in 1 Timothy 2:12 to maintain order and decorum in worship services, not to prevent women from holding positions of leadership.[82]

In her analysis of these controversial passages in Paul's writings, Sarah clearly enunciated her views on the subject of women serving as leaders in the church. She wrote:

> I think we must be compelled to adopt one of two conclusions; either that the apostle grossly contradicts himself on a subject of great practical importance, and the fulfillment of the prophecy of Joel was a shameful infringement of decency and order; or that the directions given to women, not to speak, or to teach in the congregations, had reference to some local and peculiar customs, which were then common in religious assemblies, and which the apostle thought inconsistent with the purpose for which they were met together.[83]

---

[81]Ibid., 95.

[82]Ibid.

[83]Ibid. Sarah's citation of the prophecy of Joel is a reference to Joel 2:27–29, in which the prophet declares: "But this is that which was spoken by the prophet Joel, 'And it shall come to pass in the last days, saith God, I will pour out of my Spirit upon all flesh, and your sons and your daughters shall prophesy, and your young men shall see visions, and your old men shall dream dreams. And on my servants and on my handmaidens I will pour out in those days of my Spirit; and they shall prophesy.'" In his sermon at Pentecost, Peter quoted from Joel's prophecy (Acts 2:16–17).

A final controversial issue with which Sarah dealt as she examined Paul's writings on women was the issue of the proper husband-wife relationship. The traditional position promoted a hierarchical structure governed the husband-wife relationship. Proponents of male superiority pointed to verses such as Ephesians 5:23, which reads: "The husband is the head of the wife, even as Christ is the head of the Church." In response to those who held this view, Sarah remarked that God and Christ are one and where there is "no inferiority there is no divisibility."[84] One may infer from Sarah's remarks that she found no justification for male superiority in Paul's statement. In her further comments on the Ephesian passage, she argued that woman is "the image of God, inasmuch as she is the image of man."[85] She referred to the work of commentators, including Matthew Henry, who believed women to be on the same level as animals, that is, women were created solely to help and to comfort men. Sarah countered such an interpretation by writing that "the idea that man, as man, is superior to woman, involves an absurdity so gross, that I really wonder how any man of reflection can receive it as of divine origin; and I can only account for it, by that passion for supremacy, which characterizes man as a corrupt and fallen creature."[86] Sarah contended that acceptance of a belief in a divine hierarchy in the husband-wife relationship meant that a man must bear the burden of a woman's sin and must assume responsibility for her salvation. Most men, however, were neither willing nor able to assume such an incredible responsibility.[87]

After offering criticism of long-held biblical interpretations, Sarah recognized that she must provide a new scriptural interpretation. In her analysis of scripture, she had already begun offering this new hermeneutic. Throughout her letters, Sarah had suggested alternative translations and explanations of favorite proof

---

[84]Ibid., 82.
[85]Ibid.
[86]Ibid., 83.
[87]Ibid., 85.

texts for women's subordination, and now she was ready to set forth a biblical basis for her understanding of gender equality. This task was not a difficult one for Sarah because of her background within the Society of Friends. The Quakers had provided her with a strong biblical foundation for the egalitarian treatment of women, and Sarah drew heavily from the work of Quaker scholars who years before had challenged the traditional views on the proper sphere for women.[88]

Like the Society of Friends, Sarah built her defense of female equality on Galatians 3:28, which reads, "There is neither Jew nor Greek, there is neither bond nor free, there is neither male nor female: for ye are all one in Jesus Christ." Using this verse as her support, Sarah argued that no distinctions must exist among Christian people. All persons were equal because all had been brought together in unity by God. Yet Sarah recognized that women were not fulfilling this God-instituted design, and she believed that it was impossible for any woman to "fill the station assigned her by God, until her brethren mingle with her as a equal, as a moral being."[89] Sarah asserted that until Galatians 3:28 is implemented, "we never can derive that benefit from each other's society which it is the design of our Creator that we should."[90] Sarah then called women to "claim those sacred and inalienable rights, as a moral and responsible being, with which her Creator has invested her."[91]

In addition to offering a new feminist interpretation of the Bible, Sarah, in her *Letters on the Equality of Sexes*, also examined the condition of women in other areas of the world and reviewed the contributions of women throughout history. Much of the information she used was based on outside sources, including Lydia Child's *History of the Condition of Women, in Various Ages and Nations*. At points, Sarah quoted lengthy passages of this work.

---

[88]Gifford, "American Women and the Bible," 20.
[89]Grimké, *Letters on the Equality of the Sexes*, 42.
[90]Ibid.
[91]Ibid.

Child's influence also is seen in Sarah's writings as she discussed the treatment received by women in Asia, Africa, and Europe.[92]

Another feature of the *Letters on the Equality of the Sexes* is its inclusion of a comprehensive list of successful women—great women of the Bible, women intellectuals, women ministers, and women rulers. By offering a brief presentation of the achievements of women throughout history, Sarah hoped to correct the view that women were inferior and had always been inferior to men. Her list allowed her the opportunity to argue that numerous women in the past, despite many difficulties and limitations, had contributed significantly to the world.[93]

In the sections on biblical interpretation as well as in the sections on the status and treatment of women, one theme prevails in Sarah's *Letters on the Equality of the Sexes*: the need for full equality for women. This call for full equality in the 1830s came at a time when industrialization and urbanization were expanding the vocational and economical opportunities for the average middle-class man. For women during this period, the opposite was true. Many of their traditional functions, including spinning, weaving, and soap-making, began to be performed outside the home in factories. As a result, the sphere of influence for women narrowed to what has been called "domesticity," that is, housekeeping, childcare, and entertaining.[94]

The "cult of domesticity," as Nancy Cott has identified the nineteenth-century understanding of the appropriate sphere for women, supported the view of female subordination.[95] The role of

---

[92]Carolyn I. Karcher, *The First Woman of the Republic: A Cultural Biography of Lydia Maria Child* (Durham NC: Duke University Press, 1994) 225.

[93]Grimké, *Letters on the Equality of the Sexes*, 62–67, 87–92.

[94]Barbara Leslie Epstein, *The Politics of Domesticity: Women, Evangelism, and Temperance in Nineteenth-Century America* (Middletown CT: Wesleyan University Press, 1981) 76.

[95]Nancy Cott, *The Bonds of Womanhood: "Woman's Sphere in New England, 1780–1835"* (New Haven: Yale University Press, 1977).

women was to serve men within the home. Thus, women were expected to make their homes a calm and peaceful refuge from the competitive world for their husbands.[96] As a result of such an emphasis, female education centered on training girls to be better companions to men and to be better mothers to sons. Freedom from these expectations did not exist even for those "unfortunate" women who had to work outside the home. Any wages they earned and any personal property they acquired belonged to their husbands.[97]

Such legal and social discrimination characterized the condition of women during the period in which Sarah wrote her *Letters on the Equality of the Sexes*. She used her insight into the condition of women to support her call for full equality of the sexes in the area of education. Sarah contended that any intellectual or moral weakness found in women resulted from the repression of female educational opportunities. Sarah believed that she had been the victim of such repression. The educational restrictions placed on her by her father and her older brother led her to write, "The powers of my mind have never been allowed expansion; in childhood they were repressed by the false idea that a girl need not have the education I coveted."[98]

From early childhood, girls learned "to regard marriage as the one thing needful, the only avenue of distinction."[99] Sarah argued that such an emphasis on marriage and the traditional custom of men initiating marriage proposals caused women to accentuate characteristics that men found attractive and to suppress characteristics that men found threatening or unfeminine. As a result, women repressed their intellectual development because they believed that men disliked intelligent women. Men, therefore,

---

[96]Ibid., 21, 64–67.

[97]Bartlett, Introduction to *Letters on the Equality of the Sexes*, 12.

[98]Sarah Grimké to Harriot Hunt, 31 December 1852, Weld-Grimké Collection, William L. Clements Library, University of Michigan, Ann Arbor.

[99]Grimké, *Letters on the Equality of the Sexes*, 56.

regarded women as "pretty toys or as mere instruments of pleasure."[100]

Sarah concluded that the belief that marriage should be the goal of all women led them to tolerate unequal educational opportunities.[101] In an attempt to rectify the lack of educational opportunities for women, she suggested that male students abandon their dependence on the generosity and hard work of women to support their educational goals.[102] The discontinuation of such a practice would free women to purchase books for themselves, thereby expanding their "useful knowledge." Sarah concluded: "If the minds of women were enlightened and improved, the domestic circle would be more frequently refreshed by intelligent conversation, a means of edification now deplorably neglected, for want of that cultivation which these intellectual advantages would confer."[103] Women, however, could not depend on men to provide them with or to encourage them in their educational goals. Sarah challenged women to take a more active role in the area of education. Such a role was not merely a choice but a duty for women. According to Sarah, women could achieve educational equality, but to do so, they would have to depend on the guidance and assistance of God.[104]

Sarah's advice to women to rely on God rather than men in their attempts to acquire an education is unexpected given her own educational pilgrimage. Early in her life, her learning experiences were guided by her brother Thomas. Later, Quaker men such as Israel Morris supported her desire to broaden her educational horizons and also contributed the reading materials that led to her adoption of the Quaker faith. In her years as a public abolitionist worker, William Lloyd Garrison and Henry Wright encouraged her in all her attempts to obtain further training and education. Instead

---

[100]Ibid., 57.
[101]Scott, *The Southern Lady*, 62.
[102]Grimké, *Letters on the Equality of the Sexes*, 99.
[103]Ibid.
[104]Ibid., 99–100.

of looking to her own experience, Sarah seemingly based her advice on her perception that most women's educational goals were hampered rather than helped by the men around them.

If women were to secure equal educational opportunities, then, according to Sarah, they would eventually attain vocational equality as well. Vocational equality meant that women could work alongside men in the occupation of their choice.[105] Sarah emphatically expressed her convictions about the proper role of women by stating, "WHATSOEVER IT IS MORALLY RIGHT FOR A MAN TO DO, IT IS MORALLY RIGHT FOR A WOMAN TO DO."[106] The only vocation that Sarah considered improper for women was that of politician. She encouraged women to avoid becoming involved in politics because such involvement would only immerse them "in the guilt which appears to be inseparable from political affairs"[107]

In all other areas, however, Sarah called for vocational equality. She argued that women in the medieval period had been able to fulfill their vocational callings: "Women preached in public, supported controversies, published and defended theses, filled the chairs of philosophy and law, harangued the popes in Latin, wrote Greek and read Hebrew. Nuns wrote poetry, women of rank became divines."[108] She observed that in the more recent past, gifted and learned women had been professors, lawyers, and authors. These avenues, Sarah insisted, once again must be opened to women. Yet her own personal goals colored her defense of vocational equality. Because of her commitment to serve as a minister, her defense of

---

[105]Ibid., 36, 57.

[106]Ibid., 100. Emphasis is Sarah's.

[107]Ibid., 48.

[108]Ibid., 66. Sarah's examples, however, reflect a small minority of women who gained vocational equality in the Middle Ages. See Frances and Joseph Gies, *Women in the Middle Ages* (New York: Crowell, 1978) and Angela M. Lucas, *Women in the Middle Ages: Religion, Marriage, and Letters* (New York: St. Martin's Press, 1983).

women gaining access to all vocations is devoted almost exclusively to the right of women to assume the role of minister.

Sarah's earlier statements about the necessity of allowing women to serve as Christian ministers had met with great protest. Male ministers, who felt threatened by the idea of female ministers, defended their "right" to spiritual superiority and advised Sarah that only men were strong enough to deal with the ultimate issues of life and death.[109] Sarah did not ignore such criticism. In *Letters on the Equality of the Sexes*, she repeatedly maintained that women could deal with the issues of sin and salvation.[110] She pointed to the Old Testament practice of women acting as prophetesses:

> That women were called to the prophetic office, I believe is universally admitted. Miriam, Deborah, and Huldah were prophetesses.... And if Christian ministers are, as I apprehend, successors of the prophets...then of course, women are now called to that office as well as men, because God has no where withdrawn from them the privilege of doing what is the great business of preachers, viz. to point the penitent sinner to the Redeemer.[111]

For Sarah, the ministries of Philip's daughters, Priscilla, and Phoebe described in the New Testament further substantiated the biblical mandate for women to hold positions of spiritual leadership.[112]

In her defense of female ministers, Sarah relied heavily on "rights" language. She inferred that women, like men, have a right to pursue the ministry if that was their chosen vocation. Yet Sarah failed to acknowledge that ministry is not a right for either men or women. It is a vocation that comes only by divine calling and by the

---

[109]Judith Nies, *Seven Women: Portraits from the American Radical Tradition* (New York: Viking Press, 1977) 22.

[110]Ibid.

[111]Grimké, *Letters on the Equality of the Sexes*, 87.

[112]Ibid., 91, 97–98.

outward affirmation of a community of faith. Thomas Oden offers insight as to why the issue of women in ministry may not simply be understood as a civil right, "analogous to other employment, to which equal access is rightly due." He contends:

> It is an important assumption of religious liberty that ordination is not a civil right, that is, it is not under government authority, but rather, is a solemn rite of the believing community. Ordination exists only by divine calling and by the outward affirmation of the believing community. So the question of whether women should be or are capable of being ordained to ministry requires a theological, not merely a legal, answer or investigation. It is not merely a question of civil law, it is a question of sound theological, exegetical, and historical reflection.[113]

Sarah's use of "rights" language in reference to women ministers, therefore, does not seem to be in keeping with the biblical emphasis on ministry as an opportunity given by God and endorsed by the church.

Sarah also applied "rights" language to the inability of women to gain educational and vocational equality. She concluded that the lack of educational and vocational equality was directly attributable to the bias of the legal system, and she maintained that a significant number of laws had been enacted in an effort to destroy women's independence and to crush their individuality. Ironically, women had had absolutely no voice in establishing the laws that were designed to govern them. This situation, according to Sarah, robbed women of their essential rights and caused them to be treated as slaves rather than as citizens. Sarah proclaimed:

---

[113]Thomas C. Oden, *Pastoral Theology: Essentials of Ministry* (San Francisco: Harper & Row, 1983) 37.

The very being of a woman, like that of a slave, is absorbed in her master. All contracts made with her, like those made with slaves by their owners, are a mere nullity. Our kind defenders have legislated away almost all our legal rights, and in the true spirit of such injustice and oppression, have kept us in ignorance of those very laws by which we are governed. They have persuaded us, that we have no right to investigate the laws, and that, if we did, we could not comprehend them.[114]

The legal inequality women faced, Sarah argued, resulted from male control of the legal system. She wrote, "The laws which have generally been adopted in the United States, for the government of women, have been framed almost entirely for the exclusive benefit of men, and with a design to oppress women."[115] Only when such laws were annulled would women occupy the exalted station to which they were intended by their Maker to hold. It seems ironic that Sarah's condemnation of the legal system of her day was not accompanied by a call to action. Instead of encouraging women to involve themselves in the political system in order to reform its abuses, she condoned their lack of involvement in politics.

The lack of equality for women in the areas of education, vocation, and the law, according to Sarah, resulted in women being denied economic equality. Without proper educational opportunities, vocational choices, and legal protection, women could not possibility expect to gain financial independence. The economic oppression women suffered was especially evident in the lives of working women of the lower socioeconomic class. Many of these women had no choice but to work outside the home, yet they received lower pay than their male counterparts. Sarah attributed this inequity to the "disproportionate value set on the time and labor of men and of women."[116] Examples of inequity included: male

---

[114]Ibid., 72.

[115]Ibid., 76.

[116]Ibid., 59.

teachers received a higher tuition than female teachers, male tailors earned two to three times more than female tailors for doing the same tasks, and male laborers made twice as much as female laborers even though the women worked as hard in proportion to the men.[117] As a result of continued economic oppression, Sarah argued that most women assumed such inequity to be appropriate, that is, they believed they deserved less pay than men. Sarah further contended that economic inequity caused women "to regard themselves as inferior creatures."[118] Economic inequality, therefore, destroyed women's self-respect and diminished their capacity to retaliate against the injustices of the social structure.

Sarah's emphasis on full equality for women in her *Letters on the Equality of the Sexes* marked a new departure in the development of the women's rights issue during the nineteenth century. Unlike earlier feminists, she forcefully attacked the issue of the debasement of women and the reluctance of women to oppose such debasement. She condemned the principle of masculine domination in the areas of government, church, education, and economics. She also called women to take action against the oppressive social structure.[119] Throughout the remainder of her life, Sarah continued to stress her commitment to full female equality.

The year in which Sarah's *Letters on the Equality of the Sexes* were published (1838) proved to be her last year as a public reformer. On 14 May 1838, Angelina married Theodore Weld, and following the ceremony the Welds along with Sarah retired from their public roles as abolitionists and settled into domestic life. Most conservative abolitionists endorsed this marriage. They believed that Angelina would strengthen Weld's research on slavery and that the marriage would remove Angelina and her sister from their

---

[117]Ibid.

[118]Ibid.

[119]Keith E. Melder, "Forerunners of Freedom: The Grimké Sisters in Massachusetts, 1837–38," *Essex Institute Historical Collection* 103/3 (July 1967): 239–40.

controversial role as public abolition reformers.[120] Radicals such as
Henry Wright, however, discouraged the marriage, claiming that it
would end the sisters' career as public agitators.[121] The Quakers also
disapproved of the marriage. Shortly after the wedding both Sarah
and Angelina received formal notices of their disownment from the
Society of Friends. The society attributed Angelina's disownment to
her marriage to a non-Quaker and Sarah's disownment to her
attendance at her sister's wedding ceremony.[122]

The most significant response to Angelina's marriage was
Sarah's. Angelina and Weld wanted her blessing, and she readily
gave it. In a letter to Weld before the wedding, Sarah wrote:

> Often have I contemplated the probability of Angelina
> being married and felt as if my whole soul shrunk from
> seeing her a wife, such as I beheld other women, for never,
> altho [sic] deeply impressed with the belief that the marriage
> institution was designed by God to perfect the happiness of
> his rational creatures, never have I seen a married pair who
> fulfilled what I believe is intended by the expression "they
> twain shall be one flesh." Thy views, thy feelings are so
> different from those of any other man whose sentiments have
> been known to me.... My spirit is refreshed to find one man
> who feels as thou dost.[123]

On 15 May, the day following the wedding ceremony, the
sisters attended the opening session of the Anti-Slavery Convention
of American Women. Both were elected to serve as vice presidents,
and both presented multiple resolutions denouncing racial prejudice,

---

[120]Eleanor Flexner, *Century of Struggle: The Woman's Rights Movement in the United States* (Cambridge MA: Belknap Press, 1959) 246.
[121]Ibid.
[122]Barnes and Dumond, *Letters of Theodore Dwight Weld*, 2:701–2.
[123]Sarah M. Grimké to Theodore Weld, 29 April 1838, in Barnes and Dumond, Letters of Theodore Dwight Weld, 2:650–51.

commending Southerners sympathetic to the cause of abolition, and applauding the efforts of British female abolitionists.[124]

Later in May, Weld and Angelina moved to Fort Lee, New Jersey, on the Hudson River. Forty-six-year old Sarah accompanied them and lived with them for most of the remainder of her life. Such a situation was not unusual for newlywed couples of the day. Unmarried sisters often lived with and interacted closely with their sisters or brothers.[125]

Despite their retirement from public reform, the sisters continued to support and to work quietly for the abolition cause. Together they circulated antislavery pamphlets in their neighborhood and encouraged their new neighbors to sign petitions. Sarah became more involved in supporting the use of free labor products and assisted in the organization of a free labor convention to be held in Philadelphia.[126] Although the sisters continued to participate in reform efforts, their lack of public appearances on behalf of abolition and women's rights gave rise to the accusation that they had abandoned these causes. While most of their critics blamed Angelina's marriage to Weld for hampering the sisters' reform careers, their "retirement" from public reform work was primarily due to the continuing schisms and growing hostility among their former colleagues.[127]

Late in 1838, male leaders of the Massachusetts Anti-Slavery Society sought to halt the participation of women in their society. Amos Phelps and other conservative abolition leaders objected to the Society's support of women speaking publicly against slavery. Female abolitionists and their supporters countered all the

---

[124]Larry Ceplair, ed., *The Public Years of Sarah and Angelina Grimké: Selected Writings, 1835–1839* (New York: Columbia University Press, 1989) 302.

[125]Bass, "The Best Hopes of the Sexes," 217.

[126]Gerda Lerner, *The Grimké Sisters from South Carolina: Pioneers for Woman's Rights and Abolition,* Studies in the Life of Women, ed. Gerda Lerner (New York: Schocken Books, 1971) 132.

[127]Ceplair, *The Public Years of Sarah and Angelina Grimké,* 325.

objections, but the controversy weakened the society.[128] In May 1839, male abolitionists presented resolutions at the American Anti-Slavery Society convention that were aimed at preventing women from being seated, speaking, and serving on committees. The resolutions failed. In that same month, the New England Anti-Slavery Society split into two separate organizations over the question of female participation. The hostility over the "woman question" even had a negative impact on the Boston Female Anti-Slavery Society. The conservative women members preferred not to continue financial support of the Massachusetts Anti-Slavery Society or *The Liberator*, both of which were considered to be too radical in terms of women's rights.

The internal quarrels among the abolitionist leaders hurt Sarah especially. For the first time in her life, she felt free to explore her vocational goals. Yet the quarrels within the abolition movement dampened her enthusiasm for continued public involvement. The fact that she had friends on both sides of the conflict also disturbed her. Rather than take sides, she refused to continue in her public reform efforts.

Sarah's decision to discontinue her role as a public figure and a leader of the abolition movement allowed her some much-needed time for rest and renewal, and she soon found that she was content with domestic life. After a year of living with hectic schedules and having great demands placed on her, she enjoyed the relaxing atmosphere and leisure time. She also began to understand her work for women's rights as that of a forerunner. In 1838, she suggested that her role had been to break new ground for women. She wrote: "I do not know but my business is simply to open doors, or do the first rough work.... At present, I feel contented & happy & grateful in our sweet retirement, which the Lord has abundantly blessed, and we all desire to use the leisure we may be favored with in acquiring further information & preparing for future usefulness."[129] Sarah had

---

[128]Lerner, *The Grimké Sisters from South Carolina*, 283.

[129]Sarah M. Grimké to Anne Warren Weston, 17 July 1838, in Grimké, *Letters on the Equality of the Sexes*, 327.

done the task of opening doors effectively. Now she believed it was time to move on to other tasks.

One task that consumed much of Sarah's time and energy was a project initiated by her brother-in-law. Weld had begun collecting and editing testimonies on slavery, and along with Angelina, Sarah served as a research and editorial assistant for the project. In a letter to Elizabeth Pease, a British Quaker, Sarah revealed the purpose for producing such a volume:

> Notwithstanding all that has been written, the public is comparatively ignorant of the sufferings of the slave, & we are every where met by the assertion that they are "well treated...." The state of our cause loudly demanded a work which would not *prove by argument* that slavery & cruelty were inseparable; but which would contain a mass of *incontrovertible facts*, that would exhibit the horrid barbarity of a system which embrutes [*sic*] Gods rational creatures.[130]

Weld, Angelina, and Sarah read hundreds of newspapers, conducted numerous interviews, and presented to the public in 1839 a pamphlet titled *American Slavery As It Is: Testimony of a Thousand Witnesses*.[131] This work became the most powerful pamphlet in antislavery literature until the publication of *Uncle Tom's Cabin*.[132] Over 100,000 copies of the pamphlet were sold in America during its first year of publication, and it was widely distributed in Great Britain.[133]

---

[130]Sarah M. Grimké to Elizabeth Pease, 10 April 1839, in Ibid., 331–32.

[131][Theodore Dwight Weld], ed. *American Slavery As It Is: Testimony of a Thousand Witnesses* (New York: American Anti-Slavery Society, 1839; reprint, New York: Arno Press, 1968).

[132]Harriet Beecher Stow's work seems to be at least partially based on the content and totally influenced by the spirit of *American Slavery As It Is*. See Lerner, *The Grimké Sisters from South Carolina*, 266.

[133]The pamphlet, published by the American Anti-Slavery Society, sold for 37¢ a copy or $25 for 100 copies. See Benjamin P. Thomas, *Theodore*

The same year in which *American Slavery As It Is* was published, Sarah produced "Letter on the Subject of Prejudice Amongst the Society of Friends in the United States." She wrote the letter in response to an appeal from Elizabeth Pease, who believed such a letter would enable British Quakers to pressure their American counterparts to end their prejudice against blacks. Sarah incorporated into this letter some of her correspondence with Sarah Douglass, a free black woman and a member of the Society of Friends. Sarah also included her own experiences of discrimination within Quaker meetings.[134]

The writing projects of 1839 exhausted Sarah. Yet, along with her sister and Weld, she continued to entertain fellow abolitionists in their home at Fort Lee and to discuss the strategies of the antislavery workers. Even the difficulties that Angelina experienced due to her first pregnancy did not stop visitors from being welcomed into the Weld home.[135] In February 1840, only two months after the birth of the Welds' first son, Charles, the family moved to Belleville, New Jersey.[136] There they continued to correspond with

---

Weld: Crusader for Freedom (New Brunswick NJ: Rutgers University Press, 1950) 172 and William H. Willimon, "The Grimké Sisters: Prophetic Pariahs," *South Carolina History Illustrated* 1/2 (May 1970): 58.

[134]Sarah Grimké, "Letter on the Subject of Prejudice Amongst the Society of Friends in the United States," 1839, Sarah Grimké Papers, Boston Public Library, Boston, MA.

[135]Lerner, *The Grimké Sisters from South Carolina*, 278.

[136]During the early years at Belleville, Angelina apparently expressed some interest in adventist views of William Miller. Lerner explains Angelina's interest "not so much as an ideological aberration, but as an emotional response to a profound crisis in Angelina's life." Angelina's poor health, a recent miscarriage, and the death of a close friend all contributed to her acceptance of prophecies of imminent disaster. See Lerner, *The Grimké Sisters from South Carolina*, 308.

Ronald Graybill, however, suggests that Millerism was more than an intellectual adventure for Angelina. He attributes her attraction to Millerism to her distrust of orthodox biblical interpretation and her yearning for personal holiness, purity, and perfection. There is no

and visit antislavery friends. The Belleville home became a shelter for homeless people and a retreat for tired and weary abolitionists.[137] To support his family, Weld established a school in which both Sarah and Angelina served as teachers and administrators. Angelina taught history, while Sarah taught French and acted as the bookkeeper.

During their years at Belleville, Angelina gave birth to two other children: Theodore (3 January 1841) and Sarah Grimké Weld (22 March 1844). Although being a mother delighted Angelina, her health deteriorated. Weld and Sarah referred to Angelina's physical ailments as "accidents" or "injuries," but her problems were most likely caused or at least aggravated by her pregnancies. Her pregnancies and the deliveries of all her children were difficult, and between the birth of her second and third children, Angelina suffered a miscarriage. The "injuries" Weld mentioned most likely referred to the suffering caused by a prolapsed uterus and a hernia, both of which caused her considerable pain. As a result of Angelina's poor health, Sarah often acted as a surrogate mother for the children, and they became the central interest in her life.[138] There is some debate as to whether Angelina's health problems were as extreme as Weld and Sarah seemed to believe they were. The two spoke of her and treated her as if she were an invalid. Angelina's health problems, however, did not prevent her from remaining both physically and mentally active. She ran her household, supervised her children, and entertained guests. Given

---

indication, however, that Sarah ever adopted any of the Millerite doctrines. See Ronald D. Graybill, "The Abolitionist-Millerite Connection," in *The Disappointed: Millerism and Millenarianism in the Nineteenth Century*, ed. Ronald L. Numbers and Jonathan M. Butler (Bloomington: Indiana University Press, 1987) 139–52.

[137]George Lowell Austin, "The Grimké Sisters: The First American Women Advocates of Abolition and Women's Rights," *The Bay State Monthly* 3/3 (August 1885): 188.

[138]Katharine Du Pre Lumpkin, *The Emancipation of Angelina Grimké* (Chapel Hill: University of North Carolina Press, 1974) 193.

her active life and the fact that she lived to the age of seventy-two, it is difficult to understand the repeated references to Angelina's poor health. Gerda Lerner believes that there was "no conscious deception here; both Sarah and Weld believed firmly in Angelina's weakness, debility and infirmity which she bore with the patience of a saint."[139]

Sarah and the Welds lived in Belleville and ran the school for thirteen years. The school never grew very large, but the responsibility and work involved in running it was more than they could handle. In 1853, Weld decided to establish a larger school by merging his school with the Raritan Bay Association. The association consisted of thirty or forty educated and cultured families who bought property and settled at Eagleswood near Perth Amboy, New Jersey. Weld took charge of the association's educational department and established the Eagleswood school as an innovative educational experiment. It was coeducational, and its curriculum included physical training and sports, moral training, and a broad liberal arts education. Among the emphases at Eagleswood was dietary reform. Students and teachers alike adopted the Grahmite diet, which called for the banning of meat, butter, and rich foods. This diet was an innovative approach to nutrition proposed by the health reformer Sylvester Graham. He suggested that hot meals be consumed only once a week. Rice, bread, raw vegetables, and fruit became the central items in the diet, and meat was rarely served. This diet was thought to be conducive to health, but it also freed women from the tasks of preparing elaborate meals in a hot kitchen.[140]

Another emphasis at Eagleswood was the introduction of new ideas and philosophies. Weld brought in speakers to address the students and their parents, and these visiting lecturers included Henry Thoreau, William Henry Channing, William Cullen Bryant,

---

[139]Lerner, *The Grimké Sisters from South Carolina*, 291.
[140]Ibid., 253.

Bronson Alcott, Horace Greeley, Henry Bellows, James Freeman Clarke, Gerrit Smith, and Octavius Frothingham.[141]

The decision to join the Raritan Association proved to be a period of crisis for both Sarah and Angelina. During the fourteen years since Angelina's marriage, Sarah had been an integral part of their lives. She took on an active role in the household, supervising much of the domestic activity and mothering the children.[142] Sarah's emotional attachment to the Weld children most likely was "excessive and unrestrained," but she justified her dominant role in the household by pointing to the ill health of her younger sister.[143] Yet Angelina's health during this period appears to have been stable. Thus, Sarah's role within the Weld home became a source of conflict for the sisters.

The Welds' financial dependence on Sarah further aggravated the situation. To join the Raritan Association, Weld had to borrow $1,000 from Sarah. The loan was in addition to the money Sarah regularly contributed to the support of the Weld household and the Belleville school. This financial dependence upon Sarah irritated Angelina, who wrote, "We have too long been the sole recipient of her bounty—this obligation has long been *painfully heavy on my heart*—and she knows it full well."[144]

The source of the conflict between the sisters was complex, having "elements of a generational conflict mixed with sibling rivalry and the inevitable domestic conflict deriving from overwork, ill health and poverty."[145] Yet at the center of the conflict may have been the fact that both sisters felt "disappointed, trapped and resentful...of the restraints placed on their ability to think and work

---

[141]Adrienne Koch, "The Significance of the Grimké Family," *Maryland Historian* 3/1 (Spring 1972): 78.

[142]Carol Murphy, "Two Desegregated Hearts," *Quaker History* 53/2 (Summer 1964): 92.

[143]Lerner, *The Feminist Thought of Sarah Grimké*, 30.

[144]Angelina Weld to Mary Grimké, 1853, quoted in Lerner, *The Grimké Sisters from South Carolina*, 319.

[145]Lerner, *The Feminist Thought of Sarah Grimké*, 30.

for the political causes in which they so fervently believed."[146] Whatever the cause of the continuing conflict, the final break came in 1853 when Angelina asked Sarah to leave the family home.

Sarah, now sixty years old, was completely on her own for the first time in her life. She traveled throughout New England visiting friends, planned the rewriting of her *Letters on the Equality of the Sexes*, and began writing essays on education, marriage, and the history of women. During this period of her life, Sarah also considered attending law school. She believed that she needed more education than she could acquire from her sporadic reading, and she also saw the law profession as a means by which she could advise and protect defenseless women.[147] After consulting a lawyer in Philadelphia about her plans, she reconsidered the idea. His negative response as well as the lack of support from her friends led her to abandon the dream of pursuing a legal education.[148] Sarah's dream to further her education was once again discouraged by men, but she did not give up her attempt to find a suitable area of study. Sarah soon began contemplating the feasibility of entering the medical profession. Medicine, she believed, would allow her the opportunity to be of some usefulness to poor women and would be "a highway of improvement to women."[149] Yet despite the encouragement she received from Sarah Douglass, who was a successful medical lecturer, Sarah never seriously attempted to gain medical training.[150]

---

[146]Ibid.

[147]Catherine Birney, *Sarah and Angelina Grimké: The First Women Advocates of Abolition and Woman's Rights* (Westport CT: Greenwood Press, Publishers, 1969) 276.

[148]Gerda Lerner, *The Female Experience: An American Documentary* (Indianapolis: Bobbs-Merrill Company, 1977) 88 and Birney, *Sarah and Angelina Grimké*, 276.

[149]Sarah Grimké to Harriot Hunt, 23 May 1855, Weld-Grimké Collection, William L. Clements Library, University of Michigan, Ann Arbor.

[150]Birney, *Sarah and Angelina Grimké*, 276–77.

The inability to find a useful profession greatly disappointed Sarah and caused her to return to a skill that she had already mastered—writing.[151] During her months away from the Weld household, Sarah devoted much of her time to the preparation of manuscripts. Her writings addressed issues dealing with women's rights and condemning the unequal treatment of women. A review of the content of four essays most likely written during this period reveals the development of Sarah's feminist thought.[152] These four essays are titled "The Education of Women," "The Condition of Women," "Marriage," and "Sisters of Charity."

In an essay titled "The Education of Women," Sarah presented her most extensive comments on the necessity of education for women and shared her own great disappointment with the minimal education she had received. The essay appeared at a time when the minimal education available to women was limited to training in domestic and maternal duties.[153] The prevalent view was that women neither needed nor appreciated greater educational opportunities. Most opponents to female education asserted that women had enough education to fulfill the duties that their roles as wives and mothers demanded and thus education for women offered no benefits.

Sarah attempted to refute this view and to explain the significance of education for women. She asserted that educational opportunities for women would provide them with greater knowledge, increased potential, and improved self-esteem. Expounding on the advantages of female education, Sarah wrote:

---

[151]Lerner, *The Feminist Thought of Sarah Grimké*, 30.

[152]Because Sarah assigned no dates to these essays, no clear chronological order may be established. Gerda Lerner, however, estimates that they were written between 1848 and 1855 and suggests that at least some of the essays may have been written in 1853 and 1854, during Sarah's time away from the Weld home. See Lerner, *The Grimké Sisters from South Carolina*, 320.

[153]Cott, *The Bonds of Womanhood*, 125.

Freedom and equality furnish a salutary discipline for the mind and open a vast field to intellectual effort. They enlarge, strengthen, and preserve the power, independence, acuteness, originality and elasticity of the mind, which can never become palsied, so long as it interests itself in Human Rights. Education furnishes the means for extensive information and widens the bounds of human experience, which embraces the past and the present.[154]

Sarah recognized that in order for female education to become a reality, financial supplements must be obtained. During her lifetime, religious denominations and the government financed male education. Sarah concluded that women would attain their highest potential only when the church and the state discontinued lavishing millions of dollars exclusively for the education of boys and young men and instead began financially supporting the education of girls and young women.[155] Yet a change in the financial arrangements seemed unlikely unless women demanded such a change. Sarah believed that women must challenge the attitude that they were "content to labor for the education of men, whilst they themselves sit down in *commendable* ignorance." Until women were able to make this change happen, Sarah believed that female education would continue to be neglected.[156]

The provision of educational opportunities for women, Sarah believed, would have many benefits. First, it would enrich home-life. An educated woman would produce a better home atmosphere where, along with a well-run household, her husband could experience a "mental feast of intellectual companionship, and to that love which heart to heart and mind to mind, in sweetest sympathy can bind. Such a woman would be an ever present divinity, shedding around her a radiance and a calm, which can only be appreciated by those who have enjoyed the rare privilege of such a

---

[154]Grimké, "The Education of Women," 117.
[155]Ibid., 112.
[156]Ibid., 113.

home, or who have virtue enough to idealize domestic happiness."[157] Second, equal education also would enlarge women's sphere of usefulness. She believed education would enrich democracy by making women better citizens, and as better citizens, they could make sounder decisions concerning the fitness of political candidates. Third, equal education would result in an increase of reform efforts. Sarah believed that women had much insight and wisdom to offer society because they had experienced the consequences of unjust laws, the oppressiveness of antiquated customs, and the humiliation of being classified as inferior persons.[158] She concluded that equality in education would free women to explore new avenues of service, enable them to evaluate their influence on society, and inspire them to reflect on the social problems of the day.[159] Fourth, Sarah believed that education would "exalt and purify women and...enlarge her means of happiness."[160] Based on these conclusions about the social benefits of female education, Sarah called upon all states to grant the same educational privileges to women as they did to men.[161]

Despite the benefits society would experience as a result of female education, opposition to equal education continued. In light of such opposition, Sarah warned her readers of the dangers of female apathy toward equality in education. She maintained that women had become satisfied with their mental paralysis and dependent existence.[162] Such a lackluster response by women to equal education, however, did not surprise Sarah. She contended that the women of her day had limited insight into their own natures. Women had been disvalued for centuries. As a result, they had come to believe in their own incompetence. They had been "used as a means to an end, and that end the comfort and pleasure of man, a

---

[157]Ibid., 114.
[158]Ibid., 124.
[159]Ibid., 119.
[160]Ibid., 122.
[161]Ibid., 121–22.
[162]Ibid., 110.

being created for *his* benefit and living like a parasite on *his* vitality."[163] Because women had been convinced that marriage was their only option for fulfillment, most became content in finding a mate and suppressing any higher goals.[164]

Because of the denial of opportunities for women to use their intellectual powers, they believed themselves to be inferior to men, and Sarah argued that most women would continue to regard themselves as inferior until they received a proper education.[165] To correct this problem, Sarah urged her female readers to voice their objections to being used as a sexual objects and to being classified as merely domestic servants.[166] Women must demand equal educational opportunities. Instead of cowering before their husbands—as slaves before their masters—Sarah stated that women must stand as those who are clothed in the truth to demand, in God's name, equality with men. She wrote, "We now demand an equal education with man, to quality us to be coworkers with him in the great drama of human life. We come before him not in fear and trembling.... We come filled with a sense of the moral sublimity of our present position."[167] In "The Education of Women," Sarah moved from resentment over her lack of educational opportunities to rebellion against men whom she believed had kept women from gaining an equal education. Her conclusion for the essay, however, was a call to women to rebel and to take up the cause and fight for the right of equal education.

In another of her essays, "The Condition of Women," Sarah advocated that women be granted full civil and political rights, with guarantees of equal education and employment. Sarah's insistence about the need of equality resulted from her observation of the plight of women during her days as an active proponent of abolition. In the late 1830s, Sarah spent much time circulating petitions

---

[163]Ibid., 118.
[164]Ibid., 114.
[165]Ibid., 117.
[166]Ibid., 116.
[167]Ibid., 117–18.

against slavery. She encountered many women who expressed a willingness to sign the petitions. Yet some of these women would not sign because their husbands would not allow them to do so. Others hesitated signing until they could gain their husbands' consent. The experience caused Sarah to "see that the condition of women and that of slaves are in many respects parallel."[168] In response to such oppression, Sarah called for the reform of the political system, and she believed that such reform would happen only when women were included in leadership of government. Because women comprised half of every social class, their involvement in government would enable all classes of persons to be represented and to have their opinions heard and their grievances addressed.[169] Sarah further asserted that women potentially held great political power because of their numbers. If women could only realize their potential, they would "produce a revolution such as the world has never yet witnessed."[170]

The emphasis in "The Condition of Women" on the need for female involvement in government contrasts the views Sarah espoused in the *Letters on the Equality of the Sexes*. In her early writings, she judged the political arena to be completely immoral and corrupt, and women who entered such a corrupt arena would endanger their moral integrity. Sarah concluded, "I had rather we should suffer any injustice or oppression, than that my sex should have any voice in the political affairs of the nation."[171] By the time she composed "The Condition of Women," nearly twenty years later, Sarah had come to believe that advancements in women's rights must come through changes in the law and that women must have a voice in these changes. Thus, her later writings reveal a progression in her thought about the proper method of overcoming injustice and oppression.

---

[168]Sarah M. Grimké, "The Condition of Women," *Letters on the Equality of the Sexes*, 130.

[169]Ibid., 129.

[170]Ibid., 132.

[171]Ibid., 76.

The change in Sarah's attitude toward female involvement in government may be attributed in part to her increasing conviction that the inclusion of women in government would result in a more competent political leadership. She strongly believed in the concept of female "moral superiority," a concept championed by most feminists of her day.[172] According to such a view, women were more capable of serving in government because of the training and experience they received as mothers.

Sarah's adoption of the "moral superiority" argument is seen clearly in the following statements:

> The acquaintance which women naturally acquire of the workings of the human heart, of the unfoldings and operations of the passions, of the affectional nature, by virtue of their office as mothers renders them peculiarly fit to select those who are to represent and watch over the interest and legislate for a Christian Community. As society is deprived of the political, civil and ecclesiastical labors of woman, it is unquestionably defrauded of a purifying influence which could not but be felt in every department of government. Let the moral character of the women of the U.S. bear testimony to their power of self-government, power more essential than any other to qualify…women to reside in our halls of legislation.[173]

These statements reflect Sarah's conclusion that the nurturing qualities of motherhood made women better leaders. Based on the belief that women were the virtuous sex, Sarah argued that they had more to offer society as leaders. Women's experience as mothers would guarantee that they would be incorruptible, moral rulers. Like so many of her male counterparts, she adopted a sexist argument in order to promote her views on the proper role of women. Despite

---

[172]Bartlett, Introduction to *Letters on the Equality of the Sexes*, 126.
[173]Grimké, "The Condition of Women," 128.

her earlier statement that Jesus' teaching contained no distinction between masculine and feminine virtues, Sarah clearly advocated a distinction in order to support her belief that women should serve in government. Thus, she could be accused of teaching, as she accused others, "the traditions of men" (or in her case, "the traditions of women") instead of teaching "the commandments of God."[174]

Sarah balanced—or perhaps contradicted—her argument that women's maternal nature enabled them to govern more effectively than men by insisting that female opportunities to serve in government would improve the feminine nature. Such service, Sarah claimed, would end women's idleness and frivolity. It would also bring an end to the preoccupation of the government with making provisions for women and would allow for the elimination of the numerous laws seeking to protect helpless and dependent women.[175]

A third essay written by Sarah, "Marriage," was produced in response to a newspaper article that claimed that the woman's movement was promoting immorality and was destroying the structure of the family.[176] She referred to this newspaper article in

---

[174]See Grimké, *Letters on the Equality of the Sexes*, 38.

[175]Grimké, "The Condition of Women," 131.

[176]The handwriting in the original manuscript of "Marriage" appears to be that of Angelina, and the archivists at the Clements Library at the University of Michigan assigned the work to her. Gerda Lerner, however, believes "Marriage" to be the work of Sarah. Lerner supports her position by pointing to the numerous parallel statements found in this writing and other writings known to have been written by Sarah. Lerner also reveals that Angelina often copied Sarah's work in order to make it more legible. Elizabeth Bartlett agrees with Lerner's assignment of authorship and concludes that Sarah's comments about female sexuality and marital relations in this essay were the product of her intimate knowledge of her sister's marriage and her discussions with Harriot Hunt, one of the first female medical doctors in the United States. See Bartlett, Introduction to *Letters on the Equality of the Sexes*, 139.

the opening sentences of her essay, and then she set forth her own views on marriage.[177] Sarah wrote:

> Marriage is a necessity of our being, because of our halfness. Every man and woman feels a profound want, which no father nor mother, no sister nor brother can fill. An indescribable longing for, and yearning after a perfect absorbing of its interest, feeling and being itself into one kindred spirit. The man feels within him a lack of the feminine element, the woman the lack of the masculine, each professing enough of the other's nature to appreciate it and seek its fullness, each in the other. Each has a deep awareness of incompleteness without the other.[178]

According to Sarah, one of the key problems that kept marriages from living up to this ideal was the lack of sexual restraint by husbands and wives. In her essay, she advocated greater sexual restraint on the part of both men and women and emphasized the right of a wife to refuse sexual intercourse. Like other feminists, Sarah believed that greater sexual restraint would end the problems that often accompanied marital relations. For example, the practice of sexual restraint would enrich the relationship between husband and wife and would allow the woman to retain some sense of dignity. She would no longer be forced to provide sex for her husband regardless of her feelings for him or her fear of becoming pregnant. The woman of her day, according to Sarah, "has been continually forced into a motherhood which she abhorred, because she knew that her children were *not* the offspring of love but of lust. Has she not in unnumbered instances felt in the deepest recesses of

---

[177]The newspaper article was published by the New York Times in the summer of 1855.

[178]Sarah M. Grimké, "Marriage," *Letters on the Equality of the Sexes*, 145.

her soul, that she was used to minister to Passion, not voluntarily to receive from her husband the chaste expression of his *love*?"[179]

Sexual restraint, Sarah further argued, also would give women control over their own bodies and their own reproductive pattern. Sarah firmly believed that women should decide when they became mothers, how often, and under what circumstances. Such control over reproduction was the right of women, especially since they alone bore responsibility for carrying unborn children and often continued to assume full responsibility for nursing and caring for children after their birth.[180] This demand that women be given control over their own bodies places Sarah far in advance of feminist thinkers of her day.[181]

Given Sarah's high view of the marital relationship, her call for sexual restraint cannot be seen as a disparagement of marriage or of human sexuality. Her essay on marriage reflects neither bitterness toward the marriage relationship nor prudeness toward sexual intimacy. Instead, Sarah championed marriage as a divinely ordained union in which both men and women find fulfillment and completeness.[182] She also endorsed marital sexuality as an expression of love and care for one's spouse, not just as a means of procreation: "For altho' the desire for children is a natural excitement to the sexual act, yet that is weak in comparison with that yearning for mutual *absorption into each other*, which alone give vitality to every true marriage, and the ceasing to have children does not and cannot destroy this deep abiding feeling."[183]

In her essay on marriage, Sarah also focused attention on two controversial topics dealing with human sexuality. First, she addressed the topic of "free love." Because many marriages of the day were marriages of convenience rather than of love, radical feminists such as Wollstonecraft and Wright espoused the position

---

[179]Ibid., 141.

[180]Ibid., 142.

[181]Lerner, *The Female Experience*, 88.

[182]Grimké, "Marriage," 145.

[183]Ibid., 149.

that the partners could find sexual fulfillment outside the marital relationship. Sarah condemned such a notion. She maintained that despite their reasons for marrying, marriage partners were bound together and must remain faithful to one another. Although she conceded that in some cases marriage partners might be forced to separate, Sarah believed that even in these cases spouses were obligated to remain pure. She concluded that acceptance of a "free love" mentality would be fatal to chastity within marriage, disastrous to home-life, and demoralizing for society.[184]

A second controversial topic addressed by Sarah was prostitution. Like many feminists of her day, Sarah understood prostitution to be the result of male domination of women. The sexual and economic oppression experienced by women, Sarah believed, often pressured young women into selling themselves. The results of this situation were the satisfaction of men's sexual desires and the economic survival of destitute women.[185]

Sarah's essay on marriage contains the common themes found in her other writings. As in most of her writing, she commented on the need for economic and legal reform. Yet this essay focused attention primarily on the need for sexual reform. "Marriage" had a more explicit and elaborate writing style than any of Sarah's other essays. Consequently, it may be seen as a culmination of her thought on sexual equality.

A final essay of Sarah's, titled "Sisters of Charity," focused on the legal system and the need to reform laws governing women, especially married women. This title apparently was taken from a British feminist Anna Jameson's 1855 work, *Sisters of Charity and the Communion of Labour: Two Lectures on the Social Employments of Women*.[186] The scattered quotations from Jameson's *Sisters of Charity* found in the essay indicate Sarah's

---

[184]Ibid., 143–44.

[185]Ibid., 141.

[186]Anna Jameson, *Sisters of Charity and the Communion of Labour: Two Lectures on the Social Employments of Women*, 3d ed. (London: Longman, Brown, and Green, 1859).

familiarity with this earlier writing.[187] Sarah's "Sisters of Charity," however, differs greatly from Jameson's work. Jameson wrote as a moderate liberal, seeking political and educational reforms for women. Sarah, on the other hand, wrote as an impassioned moral reformer and displayed an angrier and more zealous writing style.[188]

In her "Sisters of Charity," Sarah first reviewed the laws affecting women and then called for the repeal of these laws because they deprived women of their intellectual and moral autonomy. She condemned the laws as "a blasphemy against God; they invade His right to decide on the equality of Human Rights and charge him with surrendering the duties and obligations, the conscience and the will of half His intelligent creation to the caprice, selfishness and physical superiority of the other."[189] Sarah also cited the accomplishments of women as evidence of the female capability in reform efforts. She pointed to Elizabeth Fry (1780–1845), who wrote laws to improve prison regulation in England; Caroline Chisholm (1808–1877), who altered and amended emigration laws in Australia; and Mary Carpenter (1807–1877), who reformed the treatment of juvenile delinquents in England. The success of these women, Sarah argued, meant that women must be capable of producing wise legislation. Such examples should end female apathy toward assuming leadership roles. Sarah maintained that women no longer could struggle through life "with bandaged eyes, accepting the dogma of her weakness" but instead women must become self-reliant.[190]

In order for female self-reliance to become a reality, Sarah recognized that women would have to demand greater access to industrial employment. They should not be content merely to play

---

[187]See Gerda Lerner, "Comments on Lerner's Sarah M. Grimké's 'Sisters of Charity, '" *Signs* 10/4 (Summer 1985): 811–15.

[188]Bartlett, Introduction to *Letters on the Equality of the Sexes*, 154.

[189]Grimké, "Sisters of Charity," *Letters on the Equality of the Sexes*, 161.

[190]Ibid., 162.

the piano, do cross stitch, or read novels.[191] Rather, they should seek out useful occupations and widen their sphere of usefulness in society. Sarah believed that the widening of female usefulness should include the eradication of prostitution and the termination of discrimination in employment. The involvement of young women in prostitution, Sarah contended, lowered the social position of all women and degraded and interfered with the sacredness of the martial relationship.[192] Discrimination in employment likewise lowered the status of all women, especially the value of their labor. To such vocational inequality Sarah responded: "Why should idle prejudice any longer shut out women from taking their place wherever intellect rather than strength is required? It will not be till the business of the world is more equally distributed that either sex will thoro'ly fulfil [*sic*] its vocation in life, or that we can hope for that harmonious cooperation which can alone make any great undertaking successful."[193] Reform of these two injustices, Sarah argued, would move women toward the equality with men that God intended them to have.

"Sisters of Charity" was perhaps Sarah's most eloquent and passionate feminist presentation. In the essay, she revealed a growing sense of sisterhood seen in her call to women to take control of their own destinies and in her acknowledgement that men can not truly understand the experiences and feelings of women.[194] She wrote, "Man never can legislate justly for woman because he has never entered the world to which she belongs."[195] Sarah's firm religious commitment also is obvious in "Sisters of Charity." Her impassioned exhortations resemble biblical exhortations. She appealed to women to discover "the divinity within" and to receive

---

[191]Ibid., 156.

[192]Ibid., 157.

[193]Ibid., 160.

[194]For further reading on the idea of sisterhood among nineteenth-century women, see Cott, *The Bonds of Womanhood*, 160–96.

[195]Grimké, "Sisters of Charity," 162.

the truth of their own selfhood "by the spirit of God."[196] Thus, in this essay Sarah continued to couch her convictions in religious language, appealing to the divine endorsement of women's rights.

The four essays produced by Sarah in the 1850s reflect an even more pronounced feminist thought than found in her *Letters on the Equality of the Sexes*. In her later writings, she especially placed emphasis on education and law as the means by which women could gain freedom and equality. The necessity of female education had always been a prominent issue in her writings. Yet, in these four essays, equal educational opportunities for women became not just an issue for Sarah, but a demand. She concluded "Sisters of Charity" by stating:

> Woman by surrendering herself to the tutelage of man may in many cases live at her ease, but she will live the life of a slave. By asserting and claiming her natural Rights she assumes the prerogative which every free intelligence ought to assume, that she is the arbiter of her own destiny, and if her soul is filled with this godlike sentiment she will strive to reflect in her life the representation of all that is pure and noble. Self-reliance only can create true and exalted women.[197]

Sarah was convinced that education would enable women to develop their intellectual abilities, to secure vocational opportunities, and to gain control over their own destines.

While Sarah had continually emphasized the need for female education, only in her later writings did she exhort women to involve themselves in politics. Advancement in women's conditions, she contended, would come only when women have a voice in the political arena. Sarah firmly believed that through education and through political involvement women could end the abuses to

---

[196]Ibid., 162–63.
[197]Ibid., 164.

which many of them were subjected. Prostitution, unwanted and often involuntary pregnancies, and the financial and emotional dependence of married women on their husbands all could be overcome if educational freedom and political equality were provided for women.

The writing of these essays during her time away from the Weld household kept Sarah busy during this difficult period of her life. Lonely and homesick for the Weld children, she contemplated returning home after only a few weeks' absence, but Angelina wrote her in March 1854 and encouraged Sarah to continue visiting with friends. Angelina also expressed her deep-rooted resentment over Sarah's close relationship with both Weld and the children. The tone of the letter, however, is not critical. Angelina assumed much of the blame for her feelings and insisted that she wanted Sarah to return eventually to live with them.[198] Sarah accepted Angelina's explanation of her desire for her sister to not yet return home. Sarah's deep attachment to the Weld children, however, led her to return home just a few months later.[199]

The conflict between Angelina and Sarah proved to be a positive experience for them. They dealt constructively with their feelings for one another and resolved the friction between them. For the remainder of their lives, they maintained a respectful and loving attitude toward one another.[200]

---

[198]Lerner, *The Grimké Sisters from South Carolina*, 324.

[199]Mark Perry, *Life Up Thy Voice,* 206. No specific dates of Sarah's departure from or return to the Weld household are available, but it appears that she was separated from Angelina for about a year, leaving sometime in 1853 and returning in mid-summer 1854.

[200]Lerner, *The Grimké Sisters from South Carolina*, 326–27.

Chapter 6

The Latter Years and Contributions
of Sarah Grimké

In 1853–1854, for a period of approximately six months to one year, Sarah Grimké lived apart from her sister Angelina. She felt it necessary to leave the comfort and security of her home due to conflict with Angelina, and during her time away from the Weld household, Sarah spent time contemplating her future, writing essays, and visiting friends. In the summer of 1854, she returned to the Weld home and spent the remainder of her life living with her sister's family.

Upon her return home, Sarah, now sixty-one years old, continued her interest in the feminist cause. She kept in touch with the woman's movement by subscribing to the early feminist papers, *The Una* and *The Lily*. She continued writing and often sent in articles to the *New York Tribune*, the *Independent*, and the *Woman's Journal*.[1] Like other feminists of the day, Sarah began wearing bloomers. The simplicity and comfort of bloomers appealed to her. They freed her of cumbersome bustles, tight stays, and layers of petticoats, and the bloomers served as a symbol of revolt against

---

[1] Catherine Birney, *Sarah and Angelina Grimké: The First Women Advocates of Abolition and Woman's Rights* (Westport CT: Greenwood Press, Publishers, 1969) 288.

senseless restrictions placed on women.[2] Her decision to adopt this new fashion style led to public ridicule and abuse, and later she discontinued wearing the bloomers for, despite the comfort of the costume, Sarah found them unattractive as well as bothersome to make.[3] She also realized that this fashion statement was not a main issue for their reform efforts and that wearing bloomers was not a worthy issue for which to fight.

Sarah soon faced a much more serious concern. Since the early 1850s, she had considered war to be the inevitable result of the conflict over slavery, and she no longer hoped for a peaceable solution.[4] When the Civil War began in 1861, Sarah endorsed it. Although she had been a lifelong pacifist, she felt she must endorse the war because it was the final and ultimate stand against slavery. Like most abolitionists, Sarah demonstrated little confidence in or respect for Abraham Lincoln. She criticized him for instigating a war aimed at saving the union rather than at abolishing slavery. In expressing her views about the motives for the war, Sarah wrote: "It is true there are some who are waging this war to make our Declaration of Independence a fact; there is a glorious band who are fighting for human rights, but the government, with Lincoln at its head, has not a heart-throb for the slave."[5]

Sarah not only demonstrated her displeasure with the Northern motives for beginning the war; she questioned the outcome of a war instigated by men with what she considered to be less than ideal motives. She concluded that Southerners would be more inclined to accept the abolition of slavery if they were allowed to bring about reform themselves. Thus, Sarah wrote, "I want the South to do her own work of emancipation. She would do it only from dire

[2]Gerda Lerner, *The Grimké Sisters from South Carolina: Pioneers for Woman's Rights and Abolition*, Studies in the Life of Women, ed. Gerda Lerner (New York: Schocken Books, 1971) 340.

[3]Katharine Du Pre Lumpkin, *The Emancipation of Angelina Grimké* (Chapel Hill: University of North Carolina Press, 1974) 207.

[4]Lerner, *The Grimké Sisters from South Carolina*, 340.

[5]Birney, *Sarah and Angelina Grimké*, 284.

necessity, but the North will do it from no higher motive, and the South will feel less exasperation if she does it herself."[6] Sarah's shrewd analysis of the political motivation of Northern leaders and her understanding of the psychological impact the war would have on the South reflect her ability to appraise the significant events of her own day.[7] Yet her statements also reveal that even after forty years away from the South, Sarah retained a sense of regional loyalty or at least a protective attitude toward Southerners.

In 1862, due to mounting financial difficulties, the Welds and Sarah left Eagleswood and the Raritan Association. Sarah especially delighted in their departure. After seven years of a communal type of living, she longed for a more home-like atmosphere. In a letter to her friend Harriot Hunt, she wrote: "Oh I do so long for a little private home, bread and water with quiet and love would be infinitely better than the penitentiary life I have had here for seven weary years."[8] The Weld household eventually settled near Boston in Fairmount, Massachusetts, a community that came to be known as Hyde Park. Sarah, Angelina, and Weld soon joined the faculty of Dio Lewis's boarding school for girls in nearby Lexington, Massachusetts.[9]

During her tenure at the boarding school, Sarah taught French and found time to translate Alphonse de Lamartine's *Joan of Arc*. She intended the translation to introduce Americans to a courageous woman who dared to lead men.[10] The publication of Sarah's

---

[6]Ibid.

[7]Lerner, *The Grimké Sisters from South Carolina*, 341.

[8]Sarah Grimké to Harriot Hunt, 19 June 1861, Weld-Grimké Collection, William L. Clements Library, University of Michigan, Ann Arbor.

[9]Lewis, an established reformer and educator, was a founder of the Women's Christian Temperance Union and the Boston Normal Institute for Physical Education. See Lerner, *The Grimké Sisters from South Carolina*, 357.

[10]Judith Nies, *Seven Women: Portraits from the American Radical Tradition* (New York: Viking Press, 1977) 29.

translation in 1867 by Adams and Company pleased her. The pleasure that this publication brought to Sarah, however, was short-lived. The same year her manuscript was published a fire destroyed Lewis's boarding school, and due to lack of funds, he chose not to rebuild. The loss of their teaching positions was painful for Sarah and the Welds. In an effort to continue teaching, they rented a small room and took in students. The arrangement satisfied Sarah, who loved spending more time at home in Hyde Park while still having the opportunity to mold young minds.[11]

Besides teaching, Sarah continued her work to end racial prejudice and inequality. Even though the goals of the abolition movement had been fulfilled by the Northern victory in the Civil War and by the emancipation of the slaves, both Sarah and Angelina knew that much work had to be done in the area of race relations. No incident demonstrates their commitment more clearly than one that occurred in February 1868. While reading an edition of the *Anti-Slavery Standard* early that month, Angelina noticed a reference to a speech made at Lincoln University in Pennsylvania by a young man named Grimké. Thinking him to be a former slave of her family, she wrote to him and inquired of his background.[12] The young man, Archibald Henry Grimké, quickly replied to Angelina's letter and disclosed that he was a former slave of her brother Henry. Archibald revealed, however, that he was not merely Henry's slave but also Henry's son.[13]

In his letter, Archibald recounted the story of his heritage and enslavement. He informed Angelina that after the death of Henry's wife, Henry lived with a slavewoman who had been his children's nurse. The slavewoman, Nancy Weston, had three sons by Henry:

---

[11]Du Pre Lumpkin, *The Emancipation of Angelina Grimké*, 215.

[12]Janet Stevenson, "A Family Divided," *American Heritage* 18/1 (April 1967): 5.

[13]Janet Stevenson based her novel *Sisters and Brothers* on the relationship between the Grimké sisters and their black nephews. See Janet Stevenson, *Sisters and Brothers: A Novel* (New York: Crown Publishers, 1966).

Archibald, Francis, and John. Despite Henry's desire that Nancy and her sons be freed in the event of his death, Henry's older children refused to free their younger half-brothers. In response to this situation, both Archibald and Francis fled the Grimké home. Archibald successfully escaped Charleston. Francis, however, was recaptured and later sold. The youngest brother, John, continued to live and to work as a slave in the home of one of his half-brothers. After the war, the two older brothers reunited and, with the assistance of a kind woman, received some education. They eventually moved North and attended Lincoln University.[14]

The news stunned Sarah and Angelina. After reading Henry's letter, Angelina went to bed and stayed there for several days. Both sisters were devastated by the knowledge that members of their own family had acted in such an abhorrent manner.[15] After grieving over the mistreatment the young men received at the hands of the Grimké family, the sisters embraced Archibald and Francis as family members. Eager to absolve themselves of the guilt they felt, Sarah and Angelina corresponded with Archibald and Francis, invited them to visit Hyde Park, and provided financial assistance for their education. These actions may have begun as a result of guilt feelings or a sense of duty, but later the sisters came to love and admire their newly discovered nephews.[16] Their nephews, however, were slow to embrace these new relationships. Archibald and Francis had encountered hostility and mistreatment in their dealings with white people, and they seemed to expect little if anything from this new acquaintance with their aunts. But over time, the brothers began to trust Sarah and Angelina, and while Archibald and Francis did not always follow the advice given by their aunts, they came to value these new relationships.[17] From the very beginning of this

---

[14]Ibid., 89–90.

[15]Dickson D. Bruce, Jr., *Archibald Grimké: Portrait of a Black Independent* (Baton Rouge/London: Louisiana State University Press, 1993) 23.

[16]Lerner, *The Grimké Sisters from South Carolina*, 361–62.

[17]Bruce, *Archibald Grimké*, 25.

relationship, Sarah and Angelina were impressed by their nephews and greatly admired the achievements of Archibald and of Francis. Both young men graduated from Lincoln University in 1870. Francis then attended Princeton Theological Seminary and later became the pastor of the 15th Street Presbyterian Church in Washington, DC, a trustee of Howard University, and a member of the American Negro Academy. Archibald stayed at Lincoln to study for his master's degree. In 1872, he enrolled at Harvard Law School and graduated two years later with an L.L.B. He then established a law practice in Boston. Later in his life, he became the editor of *The Hub*, wrote numerous pamphlets and articles calling for racial equality, produced biographies of William Lloyd Garrison and Charles Sumner, served as the United States Consul to Santo Domingo, acted as vice-president of the National Association for the Advancement of Colored People, and served as president of the American Negro Academy.[18]

Sarah's attachment to these young men was evident. She gave up purchasing "luxury" items so that she could contribute financially to their education.[19] She even went so far as to write a controversial novel about the marriage of an octoroon and a white man, hoping that the proceeds could be given to her nephews. The book did not sell, and she was forced to abandon the project. Her concern about raising money for her "Archie-fund," as she called her efforts aimed at financing the education of her nephews, did not cease until both young men completed their education.[20] Ironically, Sarah committed herself freely and completely to the financial support of her nephews despite her earlier statements calling for women to refrain from supporting the education of men. Yet her support came in the form of sacrificing luxuries, not necessities, and she did not neglect her own attempts at educating herself through

---

[18]Lerner, *The Grimké Sisters from South Carolina*, 364–65.

[19]Bruce, *Archibald Grimké*, 29–30.

[20]Lerner, *The Grimké Sisters from South Carolina*, 364. See also Gerda Lerner, "The Grimké Sisters and the Struggle Against Race Prejudice," *Journal of Negro History* 48/4 (October 1963): 290.

wide reading. Her support of her nephews also corresponded with another of her personal goals—the liberation of persons from the residual effects of enslavement.

To the very end of her life, Sarah remained active in reform efforts. At the age of seventy-seven, she became a leader in the suffrage movement. In January 1870, she accepted a position as vice-president of the Massachusetts Woman Suffrage Association. Angelina was also elected as a vice-president, and the Grimké sisters held these positions until their deaths. In February of that same year, the sisters attended Lucy Stone's lecture in Hyde Park on the need for female suffrage. Following the lecture, Sarah participated in a discussion concerning voting rights for women. As a result of this meeting, forty-two women, including Sarah and Angelina, assembled on 7 March at a caucus meeting held prior to the town election in Boston. The women cast votes at the meeting. Even though they were not official votes, the votes served as a demonstration for the citizens of Boston of the serious commitment of women to the cause of suffrage.[21]

In 1871, at the age of seventy-nine, Sarah hiked throughout the Massachusetts countryside selling copies of John Stuart Mill's "Subjection of Women."[22] The circulation of this book, she hoped, would help to end the ignorance and closed-mindedness of the women in her area. She eventually sold over 150 copies of the work to the women of Hyde Park and the surrounding communities.[23]

In winter 1872, Sarah's health began to deteriorate. She had led a long and active life, and at the age of eighty, she could no longer maintain the rigorous schedule she had established for herself. She was no longer teaching, and after suffering several fainting spells

---

[21]Birney, *Sarah and Angelina Grimké*, 296–97. See also Lerner, *The Grimké Sisters from South Carolina*, 366.

[22]Lerner, *The Female Experience*, 88.

[23]Ibid., 89. Sarah's feminist arguments were bolder than those of Mill. While he called upon women to work for reform for the sake of better marriages and a better society, Sarah urged women to advance their condition for their own sakes.

that winter, her long walks across the countryside selling books and visiting invalids came to an end.

Sarah faced her declining health with the grace and courage with which she had met difficulties throughout her life. In the last months of her life, she wrote: "My days of active usefulness are over; but there is a passive work to be done, far harder than actual work,—namely, to exercise patience and study humble resignation to the will of God, whatever that may be. Thanks be to Him, I have not yet felt like complaining; nay, verily, the song of my heart is, Who so blest as I?"[24] Sarah suffered several severe fainting spells in August of 1873. The resulting pain and feebleness left her practically an invalid. She recovered some strength during the cooler months of the winter, but in mid-December she caught a cold, which in her weakened condition left her bedridden. Two weeks later, on 23 December, she died with Angelina at her side.

To allow her many friends and fellow reform workers to attend Sarah's funeral, it was delayed until 27 December. The Reverend Francis Williams, pastor of the Unitarian Church of Hyde Park, and William Lloyd Garrison presided at the funeral service. Garrison spoke of Sarah's lifelong commitment to end human suffering wherever she found it. He concluded that Sarah's death was "the consummation of a long life, well rounded with charitable deeds, active sympathies, toils, loving ministrations, grand testimonies, and nobly self-sacrificing endeavors. She lived only to do good, neither seeking nor desiring to be known, ever unselfish, unobtrusive, compassionate, and loving, dwelling in God and God in her."[25]

The lifelong goal of Sarah Moore Grimké was to become "a useful member of society." She struggled continually to meet that goal and was often restricted or even denied in her attempts. Yet this passionate desire to prove herself useful drove Sarah to search for a place of ministry and contribution, and in her quest for meaning and

---

[24]Sarah Grimké to a friend, March 1873, quoted in Birney, *Sarah and Angelina Grimké*, 300.

[25]William Lloyd Garrison, Funeral Sermon, December 27, 1873, quoted in Birney, *Sarah and Angelina Grimké*, 307.

fulfillment, she discovered the Society of Friends. Within the Society, Sarah at last was able to understand and to articulate her call to ministry. The tenets espoused by the Quaker community made this an ideal place for Sarah to further develop her vocation. Unfortunately, the Quaker doctrines differed from Quaker reality. Even though Quakers taught that women should be allowed an equal role within the church's government and discipline, men in fact exercised far greater policymaking and disciplinary powers in the society. She also found that the Society of Friends in the 1820s and 1830s was a closed, inbred community. As a result, it was nearly impossible for her to integrate fully into the Quaker community. Finally, Sarah's inadvertent involvement in a Quaker rift between the Orthodox members and the Hicksite members hampered, if not destroyed, her hopes of becoming a minister. In the end, her attempt to be a Quaker minister, like her childhood attempt to become a lawyer, was rejected.

Sarah eventually overcame such rejections. Despite her increasing conviction that she would never be a useful member of society, she finally fulfilled her sense of calling in 1836. That year she joined forces with male abolitionists in an effort to bring about the immediate emancipation of slaves. Sarah finally had discovered an outlet for her dream of making a contribution to society. Along with Angelina, she became the first female abolitionist agent of the American Anti-Slavery Society, and together they traveled throughout New England championing the cause of abolition. They lectured on the evils of slavery and the need to end racial prejudice both in the North and the South. Sarah's attention to the humiliating and demeaning treatment received by slaves and free blacks reminded her of the treatment she had received from her family, the church, and society as a whole. Her independence and freedom also had been limited. By 1837, her lectures and writings incorporated the image of a woman kneeling in chains alongside a black man kneeling in chains. Thus, Sarah blazed a trail from abolitionism to feminism.

The depth of Sarah's religious commitment had compelled her toward involvement in the anti-slavery movement, and eventually her faith compelled her to provide biblical support for female equality. Her attempt to provide such support is found in her *Letters on the Equality of the Sexes and the Condition of Women*. In this collection of letters, she confronted the problem of biblical hermeneutics at its root. Sarah argued that the Bible had been incorrectly translated and misinterpreted, and she set out to present her own interpretation of scripture. The foundational understanding for her biblical interpretation was that men and women were of equal worth because both were created in the image of God, and based on this truth, she offered her own explanations about various scriptural passages that dealt with the role of women, and in doing so, Sarah became one of the first Americans to provide a biblical challenge to the treatment of women and to the limited roles and opportunities offered to them.

In the last twenty years of her life, Sarah continued to write. She produced a number of essays on marriage, female education, and the legal and financial status of women. These essays reveal that she was far ahead of her time. Themes found in these essays reflect what is today called sex-role indoctrination in which women have been limited to specific vocational roles and thereby to limited opportunities. Furthermore, sex-role indoctrination means that women have been taught, encouraged, and even coerced into believing themselves to be inferior.[26] Sarah denounced such beliefs as having detrimental consequences for the self-confidence and self-respect of women and for damaging society as a whole. To counter such destructive thinking, Sarah repeatedly and vigorously stressed the need for female autonomy and self-definition.

The impact of Sarah's message of female equality is difficult to measure. In her own day, she spoke to well over 40,000 people while touring New England with Angelina. Her presence on a public

---

[26]Gerda Lerner, "Sarah M. Grimké's 'Sisters of Charity,'" *Signs* 1/1 (Autumn 1975): 248.

platform alone caused many people to question their attitudes about women's roles and rights. The wide circulation of *Letters on the Equality of the Sexes* among Americans and the British is a further indication of Sarah's significance to the women and men of her day.[27]

Sarah's significance to the women of her day is seen in the influence that her actions and writings had on younger women such as Elizabeth Cady Stanton, Abby Kelly, Lucy Stone, Matilda Gage, and Susan B. Anthony, all of whom became leaders of the women's movement. Because of Sarah's influence on these women, she was listed as one of the eighteen women to whom Stanton, Anthony, and Gage dedicated their pioneering account of the woman suffrage movement, *History of Woman Suffrage*.[28] Sarah made an enormous impact on these women reform leaders despite the fact that her time as a public abolitionist and defender of women's rights had been brief and limited. Few of these women heard Sarah speak, but most all of them read and relied on the arguments found in her *Letters on the Equality of the Sexes*.

One woman who depended heavily on the work done by Sarah was Lucretia Mott, who relied on Sarah's *Letters on the Equality of the Sexes* when she began articulating her own response to an attack on women's equality. Mott even lifted exact phases from Sarah's work.[29] In acknowledging her indebtedness and her admiration for this volume, Mott claimed that it was "the most important work since Mary Wollstonecraft's *Rights of Women*."[30]

Another women influenced by Sarah and her writings was Lucy Stone. As a nineteen-year-old school teacher in Massachusetts, Stone heard of the condemnation of Sarah and

---

[27]Eleanor Flexner, *Century of Struggle: The Woman's Rights Movement in the United States* (Cambridge MA: Belknap Press, 1959) 344.

[28]Elizabeth Cady Stanton, Susan B. Anthony, and Matilda Joslyn Gage, *History of Woman Suffrage* (New York: Fowler and Wells, Publishers; reprint, New York: Arno Press, 1969) I:1.

[29]Nies, *Seven Women*, 24.

[30]Hersh, *Slavery of Sex,* 193.

Angelina by the Congregational ministers and read Sarah's *Letters on the Equality of the Sexes.* As a result, her sympathy for the inferior position of women in American society intensified and created a desire within her to fight such inferiority. She later described her feelings in response to the treatment received by the Grimkés: "If I had felt bound to silence before my interpretation of Scriptures, or believed that equal rights did not belong to woman, that 'pastoral letter' broke my bonds."[31] Stone wrote that Sarah's response to that pastoral letter, her *Letters on the Equality of the Sexes,* was "first rate," and she asserted that the letters within this volume "only help to confirm the resolution I had made before, to call no man my master."[32] In the 1840s, Stone became an agent of the American Anti-Slavery Society, and she used the society as a platform by which to voice her views on women's rights. Her speeches on the subject drew heavily from Sarah's argument that women were moral and responsible beings with the same God-given sphere of action and the same duties as men.

Sarah's work also inspired Elizabeth Robinson, a young Quaker from Mount Pleasant, Ohio. Although she did not have access to *Letters on the Equality of Women,* Robinson read of the Grimké sisters' abolition work and commended their efforts. She wrote, "What cause for rejoicing & surely light is being elicited from sources the most unexpected when such advocates of *Humane Rights* as Angelina E. and Sarah M. Grimké are raised up."[33] Thus, Sarah's actions, not just her writings, clarified for women such as Robinson the issue of women's rights and provided a "rallying point for sympathetic people everywhere."[34]

---

[31]Lucy Stone, quoted in Ibid., 193–94.

[32]Ibid.

[33]Elizabeth Robinson to Lucy M. Wright, 1 January 1838, quoted in Keith E. Melder, "Forerunners of Freedom: The Grimké Sisters in Massachusetts, 1837–38," *Essex Institute Historical Collection* 103/3 (July 1967): 240–41. Emphasis is Robinson's.

[34]Ibid., 240–41.

Sarah's influence also may be seen in the speeches and writings of Elizabeth Cady Stanton, the woman perhaps most instrumental in articulating the rights of women and of organizing Women's Rights Conventions in the late nineteenth century. In refuting the position that women should be subordinate to men, Stanton relied on Sarah's biblical analysis of male superiority. She valued Sarah's insight into scripture so much that she incorporated much of Sarah's exegesis in the publication in 1898 of her controversial *Woman's Bible*.[35]

Sarah's defense of women's rights became a foundation for the development of other nineteenth-century feminists' ideology. In *Letters on the Equality of the Sexes*, Sarah provided for feminists an image of woman as God's active moral agent, a theme found throughout the feminist writings in the decades that followed. She also articulated in her writing the basic questions of human equality that continued to be explored during the remainder of the century.

The woman who most clearly illustrated the appreciation that nineteenth-century women had for Sarah's work was Harriot Kezia Hunt. Hunt was the first female medical practitioner in the United States.[36] In 1856, she wrote her autobiography and dedicated it to Sarah:

---

[35]Nies, *Seven Women*, 24. Published in two volumes in 1895 and 1898, the *Woman's Bible* contains selections from the King James Version of the Bible followed by commentaries on the text. These commentaries focused on sections of the Bible that mention women. The intent of the *Woman's Bible* was to correct the prevalent anti-female interpretation of scripture. The contributors to this work believed that by doing this, they could remove a major obstacle to women's attempt to obtain equality. The *Woman's Bible*, although controversial, became a bestseller and was reprinted seven times.

[36]Hunt trained privately with a British medical practitioner. In 1835, she opened an office in Boston, where she practiced an unorthodox system of medicine: homeopathy and psychotherapy. In 1847, Harvard Medical College refused her application for admission. Six years later the Philadelphia Female Medical College granted her an honorary degree.

You have elevated, deepened, and brightened my public life, by your high-toned principles, leading me ever to apply the touchstone of truth to every subject, reckoning nothing small. The reforms of the day, in your philosophic mind, have been so united with gentleness and tenderness, and you have so taught me to control the impulses of my nature in the withholding of great truths, until the fulness [*sic*] of time, when like ripened fruits they could fall into wanting and waiting hands, that I have sometimes thought you a wise magician.

Your moral courage in living out the internal, is so blended with your religious responsibilities, that harmony has a meaning when applied to you.... As a woman, rare and true, you have done much for me, and also for every woman engaged in the reforms of the day.[37]

Hunt's admiration echoed that of many of Sarah's female friends and acquaintances.

Sarah's activities and her writings continue to have significance for twentieth-century Americans. A close reading of her biblical exegesis and her conclusions about the role of women in the home, the church, and the community reveals that her thinking was far ahead of most of her contemporaries, and in fact, her hermeneutical principles bear a remarkable resemblance to those offered not only by present-day feminist theologians and scholars, but by some evangelicals as well. Feminists who have offered interpretations similar to those of Sarah on the proper roles of women both in society and in the church include Elizabeth Schussler Fiorenza, Rosemary Radford Ruether, and Letty Russell.[38]

---

[37]Harriot K. Hunt, *Glances and Glimpses; or Fifty Years Social, Including Twenty Years Professional Life* (Boston: John J. Jewett and Co., 1856) vii.

[38]See Elizabeth Schussler Fiorenza, *Bread, Not Stone: The Challenge of Feminist Biblical Interpretation* (Boston: Beacon Press, 1984) and *But She Said: Feminist Practices of Biblical Interpretation* (Boston: Beacon Press,

Of these feminists, the one in whose work and writing Sarah's influence is most clearly seen is Ruether. While Ruether may not have relied on Sarah in constructing her feminist theology, she is aware of the writings of Sarah, and she places Sarah among "the first to formulate clearly the theology of liberal feminism."[39] Evangelical theologians and biblical scholars also have offered interpretations similar to those of Sarah, including Gilbert Bilezikian, Stanley Grenz, Gordon Fee, Catherine Clark Kroeger, and Craig Keener.[40] Although Sarah's work may not have directly influenced either feminist or evangelical interpretations of scripture, she was thinking and writing over 150 years ago much of what is now being thought and written

The importance of Sarah's writings, and especially her *Letters on the Equality of the Sexes*, for current day biblical, sociological, and political studies is confirmed by the fact that the collection has been reprinted twice in recent years, once in 1988 and again in

---

1992); Rosemary Radford Ruether, *Womanguides: Readings Toward a Feminist Theology* (Boston: Beacon Press, 1985) and *Women and Redemption: A Theological History* (Minneapolis MN: Fortress Press, 1998); and Letty Russell, *Human Liberation in a Feminist Perspective: A Theology* (Philadelphia: Westminster Press, 1974) and *Church in the Round: Feminist Interpretation of the Church* (Louisville KY: Westminster/John Knox Press, 1993).

[39]Rosemary R. Ruether, "Christianity," in *Women in World Religions*, ed. Arvind Sharma (Albany NY: State University of New York Press, 1987) 229.

[40]See Gilbert Bilezikian, *Beyond Sex Roles: A Guide for the Study of Female Roles in the Bible* (Grand Rapids: Baker Book House, 1985); Stanley Grenz, *Women in the Church: A Biblical Theology of Women in Ministry* (Downers Grove IL: InterVarsity Press, 1995); Gordon Fee, *Gospel and Spirit: Issues in New Testament Hermeneutics* (Peabody MA: Hendrickson Publishers, Inc., 1991); Richard Clark Kroeger and Catherine Clark Kroeger, *I Suffer Not a Woman: Rethinking 1 Timothy 2:11–15 in Light Ancient Evidence* (Grand Rapids: Baker Book House, 1998); and Craig Keener, *Paul, Women, and Wives: Marriage and Women's Ministry in the Letters of Paul* (Peabody MA: Hendrickson Publishers, Inc., 1992).

1989.[41] Of these two recent publications, only the collection edited by Elizabeth Bartlett offers any analysis of Sarah's writings. Bartlett's analysis, however, is brief and somewhat generalized, yet her work is commendable in that it is the only book to analyze all Sarah's later essays, to trace the development of her feminist views, and to comment on the life situations that contributed to the development. Bartlett's reprint is thus extremely valuable, and her work points to the continuing influence of Sarah and to the need to continue studying and learning from Sarah.

Another example of the importance of Sarah's *Letters on the Equality of the Sexes* is the fact that her letters are now available on the internet.[42] The website, Sunshine for Women, has the letters, and there are numerous other websites that contain portions of the letters as well as other information about Sarah's life and her writings.

There is still much to be learned from Sarah Grimké. Her impressive contributions to American social reform during the 1830s were unique. She confronted racism and prejudice within society, the church, and herself, and she lived out her conviction that all persons are of equal value and worth because they are all created in the image of God. Her courage and her commitment to full racial equality continues to challenge twenty-first-century Americans as we struggle with racial prejudice. Also of continuing relevance is Sarah's reevaluation of the religious restrictions placed on women by the church and her subsequent provision of a scripturally based feminist ideology. Her words challenge the church to reexamine scripture and to seek to understand the context

---

[41]These two reprints are: Elizabeth Ann Bartlett, ed. *Letters on the Equality of the Sexes and Other Essays*, (New Haven: Yale University Press, 1988) and Larry Ceplair, ed., *The Public Years of Sarah and Angelina Grimké: Selected Writings, 1835–1839*, (New York: Columbia University Press, 1989).

[42]Sarah Grimké, "Letters on the Equality of the Sexes Addressed to Mary S. Parker, President of the Boston Female Anti-Slavery Society," http://www.pinn.net/~sunshine/book-sum/Grimké3.html, (accessed April 11, 2003.

and the meaning of difficult scriptural passages. Her commitment to finding a place of service and her persistence in searching for a place in which to minister is an encouragement to modern-day women who still seek fulfilling ministry positions. Given these and many more contributions, Sarah Moore Grimké's lifelong goal of being a "useful member of society" was surely met. Through her achievements both as an activist and a writer, Sarah more than fulfilled her goal.

Bibliography

Writings by Sarah Grimké

Barnes, Gilbert H. and Dwight L. Dumond, editors. *Letters of Theodore Dwight Weld, Angelina Grimké Weld, and Sarah Grimké, 1822–1844*. New York: Da Capo Press, 1970.

Ceplair, Larry, editor. *The Public Years of Sarah and Angelina Grimké: Selected Writings, 1835–1839*. New York: Columbia University Press, 1989.

Grimké, Sarah. Diary. 19 August 1821–14 November 1828. Weld-Grimké Collection. William L. Clements Library. University of Michigan. Ann Arbor.

———. *Letters on the Equality of the Sexes and Other Essays*. Edited by Elizabeth Ann Bartlett. New Haven: Yale University Press, 1988.

———. "Letter on the Subject of Prejudice Amongst the Society of Friends in the United States." Sarah Grimké Papers. Boston Public Library. Boston MA.

———. "Narrative and Testimony of Sarah M. Grimké." In *American Slavery as It Is: Testimony of a Thousand Witnesses*. Edited by Theodore Weld. New York: American Anti-Slavery Society, 1839. Reprint, New York: Arno Press, 1968.

Secondary Sources

Abzug, Robert H. *Passionate Liberator: Theodore Dwight Weld and the Dilemma of Reform*. New York: Oxford University Press, 1980.

Bacon, Margaret Hope. *Mothers of Feminism: The Story of Quaker Women in America*. San Francisco: Harper and Row, 1986.

Barbour, Hugh and J. William Frost. *The Quakers*. New York: Greenwood Press, 1988.

Barnes, Gilbert Hobbs. *The Antislavery Impulse: 1830–1844*. New York: D. Appleton-Century Company, 1933.

Bartlett, Elizabeth Ann. *Liberty, Equality, Sorority: The Origins and Interpretation of American Feminist Thought: Frances Wright, Sarah Grimké, and Margaret Fuller*. Brooklyn NY: Carlson Publishing Inc., 1994.

Bass, Dorothy C. "'The Best Hopes of the Sexes': The Woman Question in Garrisonian Abolitionism." Ph.D. diss. Brown University, 1980.

Berg, Barbara J. *The Remembered Gate: Origins of American Feminism, The Woman and the City, 1800–1860*. New York: Oxford University Press, 1978.

Birney, Catherine H. *Sarah and Angelina Grimké: The First American Women Advocates of Abolition and Woman's Rights*. Lee and Shepard, 1885. Reprint, Westport CT: Greenwood Press, 1969.

[Birney, James G.] *Correspondence between the Hon. F. H. Elmore, One of the South Carolina Delegation in Congress, and James G. Birney*. New York: American Anti-Slavery Society, 1838.

Birney, William. *James G. Birney and His Times: The Genesis of the Republican Party with Some Account of Abolition Movements in the South before 1828*. New York: Negro Universities Press, 1969.

Bogin, Ruth and Jean Fagan Yellin. Introduction to *The Abolitionist Sisterhood: Women's Political Culture in Antebellum America*.

Edited by Jean Fagan Yellin and John C. Van Horne. Ithaca/London: Cornell University Press, 1994.

Braithwaite, William C. *The Beginnings of Quakerism.* 2d edition Revised by Henry J. Cadbury Cambridge: University Press, 1955.

Brayshaw, A. Neave. *The Quakers: Their Story and Message.* New York: Macmillan Co., 1938.

Brekus, Catherine A. "The Revolution in the Churches: Women's Religious Activism in the Early American Republic." In *Religion and the New Republic: Faith in the Founding of America.* Edited by James H. Hutson. Lanham: Rowman & Littlefield Publishers, Inc., 2000.

Browne, Stephen Howard. *Angelina Grimké: Rhetoric, Identity, and the Radical Imagination.* Rhetoric and Public Affairs Series. East Lansing: Michigan State University Press, 2000.

Bruce, Dickson D., Jr. *Archibald Grimké: Portrait of a Black Independent.* Baton Rouge/London: Louisiana State University Press, 1993.

Bushkovitch, Mary Townsend McChesney. *The Grimké of Charleston.* Greenville SC: Southern Historical Press, Inc., 1992.

Cain, William E., editor. *William Lloyd Garrison and the Fight Against Slavery: Selections from The Liberator.* Boston/New York: Bedford Books of St. Martin's Press, 1995.

Censer, Jane Turner. *North Carolina Planters and Their Children: 1800–1860.* Baton Rouge: Louisiana State University Press, 1984.

Chapman, John Jay. *William Lloyd Garrison.* 2d edition Boston: Atlantic Monthly, 1921.

Chapman, Maria Weston. *Right or Wrong in Massachusetts.* Boston: Dow and Jackson's Anti-Slavery Press, 1839. Reprint, New York: Negro Universities Press, 1969.

Child, L. Maria. *An Appeal in Behalf of Americans Called Africans.* New York: John S. Taylor, 1836. Reprint, New York: Arno Press and New York Times, 1968.

Clinton, Catherine. *The Plantation Mistress: Woman's World in the Old South*. New York: Pantheon Books, 1982.

Cooper, Wilmer A. *A Living Faith: An Historical and Comparative Study of Quaker Beliefs*. 2d edition Richmond IN: Friends United Press, 2001.

Cott, Nancy. *The Bonds of Womanhood: "Woman's Sphere in New England, 1780–1835."* New Haven: Yale University Press, 1977.

Dillon, Merton L. *Benjamin Lundy and the Struggle for Negro Freedom*. Urbana/London: University of Illinois Press, 1966.

Doherty, Robert W. *The Hicksite Separation: A Sociological Analysis of Religious Schism in Early Nineteenth Century America*. New Brunswick NJ: Rutgers University Press, 1967.

Drake, Thomas E. *Quakers and Slavery in America*. New Haven: Yale University Press, 1950.

DuBois, Ellen Carol. *Feminism and Suffrage: The Emergence of an Independent Women's Movement in America, 1848–1869*. Ithaca: Cornell University Press, 1978.

Dumond, Dwight Lowell. *Antislavery Origins of the Civil War in the United States*. Ann Arbor: University of Michigan Press, 1939.

———. *Antislavery: The Crusade for Freedom in America*. Ann Arbor: University of Michigan Press, 1961.

Du Pre Lumpkin, Katharine. *The Emancipation of Angelina Grimké*. Chapel Hill: University of North Carolina Press, 1974.

Eaton, Clement. *The Civilization of the Old South: The Writings of Clement Eaton*. Edited by Albert D. Kirwan. Lexington: University of Kentucky Press, 1968.

Endy, Melvin B., Jr. "The Society of Friends." In Volume 1 of *Encyclopedia of the American Religious Experience: Studies of Traditions and Movements*. Edited by Charles H. Lippy and Peter Williams. New York: Charles Scribner's Sons, 1988.

Epstein, Barbara Leslie. *The Politics of Domesticity: Women, Evangelism, and Temperance in Nineteenth-Century America*. Middletown CT: Wesleyan University Press, 1981.

Filler, Louis. *The Crusade Against Slavery, 1830–1860*. New York: Harper and Row, 1960.

Finney, Charles Grandison. *Lectures on Revival of Religion*. Edited by William J. McLoughlin. Cambridge MA: Belknap, 1960.

Flexner, Eleanor. *Century of Struggle: The Woman's Rights Movement in the United States*. Cambridge MA: Belknap Press, 1959.

Fogel, Robert William. *Without Consent or Contract: The Rise and Fall of American Slavery*. New York: W. W. Norton and Company, 1989.

Fox, George. *The Works of George Fox*. Volume 4. New York: Isaac T. Hopper, 1831. Reprint, New York: AMS, 1975.

Frost, J. William, editor. *The Quaker Origins of Antislavery*. Norwood PA: Norwood Editions, 1980.

Frothingham, Octavius Brooks. *Gerrit Smith: A Biography*. New York: Negro Universities Press, 1969.

Garrison, Wendall P. and Francis J. Garrison. *William Lloyd Garrison: 1805–1879: The Story of His Life Told by His Children*. Volume 2. New York: The Century Co., 1885–1889.

Gay, Peter. *The Enlightenment: An Interpretation, the Rise of Modern Paganism*. New York: W. W. Norton and Co., 1966.

Gies, Frances and Joseph. *Women in the Middle Ages*. New York: Crowell, 1978.

Gifford, Carolyn De Swarte. "American Women and the Bible: The Nature of Woman as a Hermeneutical Issue." In *Feminist Perspectives on Biblical Scholarship*. Edited by Adela Yarbro Collins. Chico CA: Scholars Press, 1985.

Graybill, Ronald D. "The Abolitionist-Millerite Connection." In *The Disappointed: Millerism and Millenarianism in the Nineteenth Century*. Edited by Ronald L. Numbers and Jonathan M. Butler. Bloomington: Indiana University Press, 1987.

Hahn, Emily. *Once Upon a Pedestal*. New York: Thomas Y. Crowell Co., 1974.

Hallowell, Anna Davis. *James and Lucretia Mott: Life and Letters*. Boston: Houghton Mifflin, 1884.

Hambrick-Stowe, Charles E. *Charles G. Finney and the Spirit of American Evangelicalism*. Grand Rapids: William B. Eerdmans Publishing Company, 1996.

Hamm, Thomas D. *The Transformation of American Quakerism: Orthodox Friends, 1800–1907*. Bloomington/Indianapolis: Indiana University Press, 1988.

Hanson, Debra Gold. *Strained Sisterhood: Gender and Class in the Boston Female Anti-Slavery Society*. Amherst: University of Massachusetts Press, 1993.

Hardesty, Nancy. *Women Called to Witness: Evangelical Feminism in the Nineteenth Century*. 2d edition Knoxville: University of Tennessee Press, 1999.

Harlow, Ralph Volney. *Gerrit Smith: Philanthropist and Reformer*. New York: Henry Holt and Company, 1939.

Henry, Matthew. *Commentary on the Whole Bible*. Edited by Leslie F. Church. Grand Rapids: Zondervan Publishing House, 1961.

Hersh, Blanche Glassman. "'Am I Not a Woman and a Sister?' Abolitionist Beginning of Nineteenth-Century Feminism." In *Antislavery Reconsidered: New Perspectives on the Abolitionists*. Edited by Lewis Perry and Michael Fellmen. Baton Rouge: Louisiana State University Press, 1979.

———. *The Slavery of Sex: Feminist-Abolitionists in America*. Urbana: University of Illinois Press, 1978.

———. "To Make the World Better: Protestant Women in the Abolitionist Movement." In *Triumph over Silence: Women in Protestant History*. Edited by Richard L. Greaves. Westport CT: Greenwood Press, 1985.

Hunt, Harriot K. *Glances and Glimpses; or Fifty Years Social, Including Twenty Years Professional Life*. Boston: John J. Jewett and Co., 1856.

Ingle, H. Larry. *Quakers in Conflict: The Hicksite Reformation*. Knoxville: University of Tennessee Press, 1986.

James, Sydney V. *A People Among Peoples: Quaker Benevolence in Eighteenth-Century America*. Cambridge MA: Harvard University Press, 1963.

Jameson, Anna. *Sisters of Charity and the Communion of Labour: Two Lectures on the Social Employments of Women.* 3d edition London: Longman, Brown, and Green, 1859.

Jones, Rufus. *The Faith and Practice of Quakers.* Richmond IN: Friends United Press, 1980.

Karcher, Carolyn I. *The First Woman of the Republic: A Cultural Biography of Lydia Maria Child.* Durham NC: Duke University Press, 1994.

Kirkpatrick, Frank G. "From Shackles to Liberation: Religion, the Grimké Sisters and Dissent." In *Women, Religion, and Social Change.* Edited by Yvonne Yazbeck and Ellison Banks Findly. Albany: State University of New York Press, 1985.

Kittelson, James M. *Luther the Reformer: The Story of the Man and His Career* Minneapolis: Augsburg Publishing House, 1986.

Kraditor, Aileen S. *Means and Ends in American Abolitionism: Garrison and His Critics on Strategy and Tactics, 1834–1850.* New York: Pantheon Books, 1967.

Lerner, Gerda. *The Female Experience: An American Documentary.* Indianapolis: Bobbs-Merrill Company, 1977.

———. *The Feminist Thought of Sarah Grimké.* New York/Oxford: Oxford University Press, 1998.

———. *The Grimké Sisters From South Carolina: Pioneers for Woman's Rights and Abolition*, Studies in the Life of Women. Edited by Gerda Lerner. New York: Schocken Books, 1971.

Lucas, Angela M. *Women in the Middle Ages: Religion, Marriage, and Letters.* New York: St. Martin's Press, 1983.

Lutz, Alma. *Crusade for Freedom: Women of the Antislavery Movement.* Boston: Beacon Press, 1968.

Mack, Phyllis. "Gender and Spirituality in Early English Quakerism." In *Witnesses for Change: Quaker Women over Three Centuries.* Edited by Elisabeth Potts Brown and Susan Mosher Stuard. New Brunswick: Rutgers University Press, 1989.

Mallalieu, W. C. "Grimké, John Faucheraud." In *Dictionary of American Biography*. Edited by Allen Johnson and Dumas Malone. New York: Scribner's and Sons, 1931.

Marilley, Suzanne M. *Woman Suffrage and the Origins of Liberal Feminism in the United States, 1820–1920*. Cambridge MA: Harvard University Press, 1996.

Matthews, Glenna. "'Little Women' Who Helped Make this Great War." In *Why the Civil War Came*. Edited by Gabor S. Boritt. New York/Oxford: Oxford University Press, 1996.

————. *The Rise of Public Woman: Woman's Power and Woman's Place in the United States, 1630–1970*. New York/Oxford: Oxford University Press, 1992.

Mayeski, Marie Anne. *Women: Models of Liberation*. Kansas City MO: Sheed and Ward, 1988.

McLoughlin, William G. *Revivals, Awakenings, and Reform: An Essay on Religion and Social Change in America, 1607–1977*. Chicago History of American Religion. Edited by Martin E. Marty. Chicago: University of Chicago Press, 1978.

McPherson, Stephanie Sammartino. *Sisters Against Slavery: A Story about Sarah and Angelina Grimké*. Creative Minds Biographies. Minneapolis MN: Carolrhoda Books, 1999.

Melder, Keith E. *Beginnings of Sisterhood: The American Woman's Rights Movement, 1800–1850*. Studies in the Life of Women. Edited by Gerda Lerner. New York: Schocken Books, 1977.

Merrill, Walter M. *Against Wind and Tide: A Biography of Wm. Lloyd Garrison*. Cambridge MA: Harvard University Press, 1963.

———— and Louis Ruchames, editors. *The Letters of William Lloyd Garrison*. 2 Volumes. Cambridge MA: Belknap Press, 1971.

Miller, Annie. *Our Family Circle*. Marietta GA: Continental Book Co., 1957.

Nies, Judith. *Seven Women: Portraits from the American Radical Tradition*. New York: Viking Press, 1977.

Noll, Mark. *A History of Christianity in the United States and Canada*. Grand Rapids: William B. Eerdmans Publishing Company, 1992.

Numbers, Ronald L. and Jonathan M. Butler, editors. *The Disappointed: Millerism and Millenarianism in the Nineteenth Century*. Bloomington: Indiana University Press, 1987.

Oden, Thomas C. *Pastoral Theology: Essentials of Ministry*. San Francisco: Harper & Row, 1983.

Pease, William H. and Jane H. Pease, editors. *The Antislavery Argument*. Indianapolis: Bobbs-Merrill Co., 1965.

Penn, William. *Fruits of Solitude*. London: Northcott, 1693.

Perry, Mark. *Lift Up Thy Voice: The Grimké Family's Journey from Slaveholders to Civil Rights Leaders*. New York: Viking, 2001.

Persons, Stow. *American Minds: A History of Ideas*. Revised edition Malabar FL: Robert E. Krieger Publishing Co., 1983.

Punshon, John. *Portrait in Grey: A Short History of the Quakers*. London: Quaker Home Service, 1984.

Riegel, Robert E. *American Feminists*. Lawrence: University of Kansas Press, 1963.

Ruether, Rosemary. "Christianity." In *Women in World Religions*. Edited by Arvind Sharma. Albany: State University of New York Press, 1987.

Russell, Elbert. *The History of Quakerism*. New York: Macmillan Company, 1942.

Scott, Anne Firor. *The Southern Lady: From Pedestal to Politics, 1830–1930*. Chicago: University of Chicago Press, 1970.

Sillen, Samuel. *Women Against Slavery*. New York: Masses and Mainstream, 1955.

Soderlund, Jean R. *Quakers and Slavery: A Divided Spirit*. Princeton: Princeton University Press, 1985.

Stanton, Elizabeth Cady, Susan B. Anthony, and Matilda Joslyn Gage. *History of Woman Suffrage*. 6 Volumes. New York: Fowler and Wells, 1881-1889. Reprint, New York: Arno Press, 1969.

Staudenraus, P. J. *The African Colonization Movement, 1816–1855.*
    New York: Columbia University Press, 1961.
Stevenson, Janet. *Sisters and Brothers: A Novel.* New York: Crown
    Publishers, 1966.
Stewart, James Brewer. *Holy Warriors: The Abolitionists and
    American Slaver.* Revised edition Edited by Eric Foner. New
    York: Hill and Wang, 1996.
Stroud, George M. *A Sketch of the Laws Relating to Slavery in the
    Several States of the United States of America.* Printed by the
    author, 1856. Reprint, New York: Negro Universities Press,
    1968.
Sweet, William Warren. *Revivalism in America: Its Origin, Growth,
    and Decline.* New York: Charles Scribner's Sons, 1944.
———. *The Story of Religion in America.* New York: Harper and
    Row, 1930. Reprint, Grand Rapids: Baker Book House, 1983.
The Liberator. Microfilm. Ann Arbor, Michigan. University
    Microfilms, 1956. 9 reels 35mm. (American periodical series,
    1800-1850, 391-99).
Thomas, Benjamin P. *Theodore Weld: Crusader for Freedom.* New
    Brunswick NJ: Rutgers University Press, 1950.
Thomas, George M. *Revivalism and Cultural Change: Christianity,
    Nation Building, and the Market in the Nineteenth Century
    United States.* Chicago/London: University of Chicago Press,
    1989.
Thomas, John. *The Liberator: William Lloyd Garrison, a
    Biography.* Boston: Little, Brown, 1963.
Todras, Ellen H. *Angelina Grimké: Voice of Abolition.* North Haven
    CT: Linnet Books, 1999.
Tyler, Alice Felt. *Freedom's Ferment: Phases of American Social
    History from the Colonial Period to the Outbreak of the Civil
    War.* New York: Harper and Brothers, 1944.
Wallace, David Duncan. *South Carolina: A Short History,
    1520–1948.* Columbia: University of South Carolina Press,
    1951.

Walters, Ronald G. *The Antislavery Appeal: American Abolitionism after 1830* Baltimore: Johns Hopkins University Press, 1976.

Weiner, Marli F. *Mistresses and Slaves: Plantation Women in South Carolina, 1830–1880*. Urbana/Chicago: University of Illinois Press, 1998.

[Weld, Theodore Dwight], editor. *American Slavery As It Is: Testimony of a Thousand Witnesses*. New York: American Anti-Slavery Society, 1839. Reprint, New York: Arno Press, 1968.

———. *In Memory: Angelina Grimké Weld*. Boston: George Ellis, 1880.

Wilbanks, Charles, editor. *Walking by Faith: The Diary of Angelina Grimké, 1828–1835*. Women's Diaries and Letters of the South. Columbia: University of South Carolina Press, 2003.

Williams, Carolyn. "Racial Prejudice and Women's Rights." In *The Abolitionist Sisterhood: Women's Political Culture in Antebellum America*. Edited by Jean Fagan Yellin and John C. Van Horne. Ithaca/London: Cornell University Press, 1994.

Willimon, William and Patricia. *Turning the World Upside Down: The Story of Sarah and Angelina Grimké*. Columbia: Sandlapper Press, 1972.

Winter, Rebecca J. *The Night Cometh: Two Wealthy Evangelicals Face the Nation*. South Pasadena CA: William Carey Library, 1977.

Wollstonecraft, Mary. "A Vindication of the Rights of Women." In *The Feminist Papers: From Adams to de Beauvoir*. Edited by Alice S. Rossi. New York: Columbia University Press, 1973.

Woolman, John. *The Journal With Other Writings of John Woolman*. London: J. M. Dent and Sons, n.d.

Wyatt-Brown, Bertram. *Honor and Violence in the Old South*. New York: Oxford University Press, 1986.

———. *Lewis Tappan and the Evangelical War against Slavery*. Cleveland: The Press of Case Western Reserve University, 1969.

Yellin, Jean Fagan. *Women and Sisters: The Anti-slavery Feminists in American Culture*. New Haven: Yale University Press, 1989.

Journal Articles

Austin, George Lowell. "The Grimké Sisters: The First American Women Advocates of Abolition and Women's Rights." *The Bay State Monthly* 3/3 (August 1885): 183–89.

Davis, David Brion. "The Emergence of Immediatism in British and American Antislavery Thought." *Mississippi Valley Historical Review* 49/2 (September 1962): 209–30.

Dillon, Merton L. "The Failure of the American Abolitionists." *Journal of Southern History* 25/2 (May 1959): 159–77.

DuBois, Ellen. "Struggling into Existence: The Feminism of Sarah and Angelina Grimké." *Women: A Journal of Liberation* 1/2 (Spring 1970): 4–11.

Harrison, Beverly Wildung. "The Early Feminists and the Clergy: A Case Study in the Dynamics of Secularization." *Review and Expositor* 72/1 (Winter 1975): 41–52.

Hewitt, Nancy A. "Feminist Friends: Agrarian Quakers and the Emergence of Woman's Rights in America." *Feminist Studies* 12/1 (Spring 1986): 27–49.

Japp, Phyllis M. "Esther or Isaiah?: The Abolitionist-Feminist Rhetoric of Angelina Grimké." *Quarterly Journal of Speech* 71/3 (August 1985): 335–48.

Koch, Adrienne. "The Significance of the Grimké Family." *Maryland Historian* 3/1 (Spring 1972): 59–84.

Lerner, Gerda. "Comments on Lerner's Sarah M. Grimké's 'Sisters of Charity.'" *Signs* 10/4 (Summer 1985): 811–15.

———. "Sarah M. Grimké's 'Sisters of Charity.'" *Signs* 1/1 (Autumn 1975): 246–56.

———. "The Grimké Sisters and the Struggle Against Race Prejudice." *Journal of Negro History* 48/4 (October 1963): 277–91.

Loveland, Anne C. "Evangelicalism and 'Immediate Emancipation' in American Antislavery Thought." *Journal of Southern History* 32/2 (May 1966): 172–88.

Melder, Keith E. "Forerunners of Freedom: The Grimké Sisters in Massachusetts, 1837–38." *Essex Institute Historical Collection* 103/3 (July 1967): 223–49.

Murphy, Carol. "Two Desegregated Hearts." *Quaker History* 53/2 (Summer 1964): 87–92.

Rosenberg, Carroll Smith. "Beauty, the Beast and the Militant Woman: A Case Study in Sex Roles and Social Stress in Jacksonian America." *American Quarterly* 23/4 (October 1971): 562–84.

Ruether, Rosemary Radford. "The Subordination and Liberation of Women in Christian Theology: St. Paul and Sarah Grimké." *Soundings* 61/2 (Summer 1978): 168–81.

Ryan, Mary P. "The Power of Women's Networks: A Case Study of Female Moral Reform in Antebellum America." *Feminist Studies* 5/1 (Spring 1979): 66–86.

Stevenson, Janet. "A Family Divided." *American Heritage* 18/1 (April 1967): 4–8, 84–91.

Vielhaber, Mary E. "An Abandoned Speaking Career: Angelina Grimké." *Michigan Academician* 17/1 (Spring 1984): 59–66.

Willimon, William H. "The Grimké Sisters: Prophetic Pariahs." *South Carolina History Illustrated* 1/2 (May 1970): 15–17, 56–58.

Index